MRS BEETON
AND
MRS MARSHALL

MRS BEETON
AND
MRS MARSHALL
A Tale of Two Victorian Cooks

EMMA KAY

PEN & SWORD
HISTORY

AN IMPRINT OF PEN & SWORD BOOKS LTD.
YORKSHIRE – PHILADELPHIA

First published in Great Britain in 2023 by
PEN AND SWORD HISTORY
An imprint of
Pen & Sword Books Ltd
Yorkshire – Philadelphia

Copyright © Emma Kay, 2023

ISBN 978 1 39900 900 3

The right of Emma Kay to be identified as Author of this work has been asserted by her in accordance with the Copyright, Designs and Patents Act 1988.

A CIP catalogue record for this book is available from the British Library.

All rights reserved. No part of this book may be reproduced or transmitted in any form or by any means, electronic or mechanical including photocopying, recording or by any information storage and retrieval system, without permission from the Publisher in writing.

Typeset in Times New Roman 11/14.5 by
SJmagic DESIGN SERVICES, India.
Printed and bound in the UK by CPI Group (UK) Ltd.

Pen & Sword Books Limited incorporates the imprints of Atlas, Archaeology, Aviation, Discovery, Family History, Fiction, History, Maritime, Military, Military Classics, Politics, Select, Transport, True Crime, Air World, Frontline Publishing, Leo Cooper, Remember When, Seaforth Publishing, The Praetorian Press, Wharncliffe Local History, Wharncliffe Transport, Wharncliffe True Crime and White Owl.

For a complete list of Pen & Sword titles please contact
PEN & SWORD BOOKS LIMITED
George House, Units 12 & 13, Beevor Street, Off Pontefract Road,
Barnsley, South Yorkshire, S71 1HN, England
E-mail: enquiries@pen-and-sword.co.uk
Website: www.pen-and-sword.co.uk

or

PEN AND SWORD BOOKS
1950 Lawrence Rd, Havertown, PA 19083, USA
E-mail: uspen-and-sword@casematepublishers.com
Website: www.penandswordbooks.com

Contents

Acknowledgements		vi
Introduction		ix
Chapter 1	Agnes Bertha Marshall	1
Chapter 2	The Recipes and Innovations of Agnes Bertha Marshall	61
Chapter 3	Isabella Beeton	100
Chapter 4	The *Book of Household Management* and Other Stories	140
Chapter 5	Day-to-Day Lives, Pinner and Peers	169
Notes		183
Bibliography		195

Acknowledgements

Early on in my research for this book, I contacted a lady called Diane Spiers who I connected with on the Genealogy website Ancestry.co.uk. We got chatting and she kindly sent me a number of images capturing aspects of her late husband Anthony Haynes's collection of items relating to Agnes Bertha Marshall. Anthony, or Tony as he was known, died in March 2018. His other collection of seventeenth-century cookery books was apparently enviable.

Within his collection of memorabilia centred on Agnes there were even original copies of *The Table* magazine. Following his death, according to Tony's wishes, the whole collection was auctioned off by Dominic Winters Auctions, who ironically are based just down the road from where I live. The following is a short biography about Tony, which was important to me to include as the man who once so lovingly accumulated so much of Agnes's work and dedicated his life to sourcing old cookery texts and other culinary-related paraphernalia.

I am myself a collector of Kitchenalia and I find a great sense of joy in being able to capture small, often insignificant objects that were once so prized. Tony photographed some aspects of his collection prior to selling and it is these images that have helped me connect with Agnes in a way I wouldn't otherwise have been able to. I would never have seen a portrait photograph of Agnes or an actual recipe, opposed to one published in a book, let alone a typed recipe that has been amended in her very own handwriting, or got a genuine sense of the relationship she had with customers from her letters. In particular, her correspondence with Mrs Massey-Dawson regarding her ice cave. One wonders how many of these letters Agnes responded to personally, providing details of her products or answering other queries. One letter is dated 1893 and was found pasted into a copy of *Mrs Marshall's Book of Ices*. Agnes was well established then, why did she not have a secretary to undertake these tasks? We shall never know, but the following biography of Tony Haynes, written by his wife Diane, is my tribute to him and everything he kept safe.

Acknowledgements

Anthony Haynes 1944–2018

Always known as Tony, he was born in Birmingham in 1944; he would describe himself as a war baby. He started collecting from an early age, the usual comics and so on that entice most youngsters. Tony, however, continued to collect these comics well into the 1980s until they were stolen from his secret hiding place, the loo, and never seen again. Unable to take things home as his mother always said, 'I don't want all that old stuff in the house,' items he bought were passed on, hopefully at a profit, to anyone who would buy them. Tony left school when he was 15 and worked for most of his life as a greengrocer. Ironically, he didn't like vegetables or many fruits and would only eat potatoes, preferably mashed with lots of butter, and frozen peas.

In the late 1970s, Tony and I moved to a new house, and at the time, Tony's greengrocer shop was in a shopping precinct. The shop next door changed hands and an antique shop opened. Tony knew the owners and was a frequent visitor. One day, he came home with a wartime cookery book, which gave instructions how to make a cheap medicine chest. First you needed a grandfather clock, take off the top, knock out the works, add a shelf and paint it white. Tony was hooked and from that day, a steady stream of cookery books entered our house, making the collection he has today. Oddly, though, Tony did not cook, although he made a good omelette or scrambled eggs, but at the same time a lot of washing up!

Tony preferred to search for books in charity shops or at bookfairs, buying from book dealers' catalogues and in more recent times on eBay. For every and any purchase he made, he would carefully sweep out every page with a children's paint brush to remove any flour or debris, making sure all the pages and illustrations were where they should be, and then the book would be put on a bookcase or in a box, unlikely to be seen again.

In later years, he took more of an interest in the authors of cookery books and would often look for more information on the author's life. He had a great interest in Charles Herman Senn and collected anything he could on Senn in the *Universal Cookery and Food Association*, delving into the exhibitions and amassing a collection of the medals they issued. He admired Isabella Beeton immensely and at one time Tony desired to collect a copy of every edition of her *Book of Household Management* collection. Tony also appreciated Agnes Bertha Marshall – he always wanted one of her moulds, but never did get one.

He had a great interest in cookery schools and collected their postcards where possible. His last main collecting field was what he referred to as 'Charity Books'. These were issued by local churches, with the help of the congregation, the aim being to raise funds towards the upkeep of the church. He never thought there would be so many.

* * *

I would also like to thank Tony's wife Diane, who was so kind to respond to my messages, talk to me on the phone, and guide me through the images left behind by her husband. For this, I am ever grateful.

Thanks also go out to Bourne Hall Museum, Epsom, for sharing and letting me include numerous images relating to Isabella Beeton and her family, as well as Surrey History Centre.

Introduction

When I first set out to write this book, my opinion was fairly resolved. Agnes Bertha Marshall was a neglected heroine of the culinary world, while Isabella Beeton stood as an impostor, a usurper of far more worthy heroines. I was, to some extent, very wrong.

For years, I have maintained a slight disregard for Beeton, even shunning a beautiful old original 1920s edition of the *Book of Household Management* gifted to me by my mother-in-law, from her mother. No more – it has been removed from the glass cabinet reserved for overspill books and now resides within grabbing distance of my desk. Many people will remain divided over Beeton, even after reading this, in terms of her lack of credible experience, while others may be shocked to realise that she never composed a real recipe of her own, although this was actually the case for many cookery writers from that era. Isabella Beeton was for all intents and purposes just one giant PR exercise that ran and ran, but she was also much more than that, of course.

While there is very little information about Agnes Bertha Marshall circulating in the world, aside from *The Greatest Victorian Ice Cream Maker* and the odd chapter in relevant books about cooks and cooking, or online blog posts, there are several excellent biographies of Isabella Beeton, most notably compiled by Kathryn Hughes, Nancy Spain (Isabella's great-niece), Seara Freeman, and H. Montgomery Hyde.

The fact that so much information and primary research material in the form of letters exists within the Beeton archives actually makes the task of writing a condensed biography harder. This is one of the reasons why I chose not to include too many references to correspondence, a job which both Nancy Spain and Kathryn Hughes have already done in detail and admirably.

I intentionally tried not to rework the information already to be found in existing biographies, choosing to conduct the research process largely from scratch. Of course, all of the above-mentioned books have been referenced and read, but mostly after I had analysed the relevant available primary sources of research for myself. This has always been my way as a historian, otherwise what is the point? While you will find omissions in this book previously communicated in other texts, you will equally discover new snippets of information.

Despite their acute differences, there are many similarities between Isabella and Agnes. Both lost their fathers at a young age, both lived within a stone's throw of each other geographically, albeit thirty or so years apart, both probably came from more humble beginnings than the lifestyle they crafted for themselves, both had dominant husbands, both understood the potential for capitalising on the culinary culture which was escalating steadily throughout the nineteenth century, both liked to travel, and both realised their potential beyond the confines of domesticity and motherhood. If only they'd met. Although the circles they moved in may not have been quite so similar.

We know that Isabella collated all of her recipes from other people. She was the antithesis of Agnes, who frequently championed the fact that all her recipes were original.

The Book of Household Management opens with layers of recommendations on etiquette, on things like what to do when seated at the dining table, or when it is appropriate to call in on someone socially at home. Rules and proper form were integral to well-heeled Victorian society. This is followed by lists of individual staffing responsibilities in larger households, from butler to scullery maid, cook, and housekeeper. Recipes gained from the public then dominate the largest sections of the book.

But these manuals, combining advice on running a home with instructions on general maintenance and cooking, were not new or innovative. Writers had been compiling these types of guides for centuries. To name a few: *The English Huswife* by Gervase Markham, 1615, *The Country Housewife and Lady's Director* by Richard Bradley, 1727, *The Compleat Housewife*, Eliza Smith, 1730. Some were in A–Z form, like John Perkins's *Every Woman Her Own House-Keeper; or The Ladies' Library*, 1796, others mostly just plagiarised from one another. This was a common practice when writing recipe books and manuals for some 300 odd years.

There were specific guides like *The Innkeeper and Butler's Guide* of 1808 by John Davies, *The Complete Servant Maid* by Anne Barker in 1770,

Introduction

or the even earlier *The Queen's Closet Opened*, by W. M. of 1655, which includes medical remedies, culinary recipes and sections on candying and preserving. Culinary and medicinal recipes were often integrated together in books of the seventeenth and eighteenth centuries. By the time Mrs Beeton came to write her *Book of Household Management*, this type of genre in many forms was very popular. Other nineteenth-century examples include *Good Form in England, The Gentleman's House or How To Plan English Residencies, Household Work, or the Duty of Female Servants, The Family Manual and Servant's Guide, Domestic Management: The Practice of Cookery Adapted to the Business of Every Day Life*, and so on.

Undoubtedly it would have been all these books, combined with Isabella's own upbringing and child-rearing experience, that would have inspired the content of her famous handbook. Earlier cookery books often included menu suggestions and table plans using basic diagrams to indicate where each dish should be placed during a meal, something which continued into the nineteenth century, also adopted by Beeton. It was popular at one stage to write whole sections on food for 'invalids' and for children. Isabella absorbed all of these elements of domestic care, housekeeping, nurturing, wellbeing, popular recipes, and etiquette to form one great big book that contained an amalgamation of many similar guides and ideas on the economies and practicalities of running a home and caring for a family that had been circulating for years.

I think it is for this and her contribution to the broader lifestyle field of the Victorian periodical *The Englishwoman's Domestic Magazine* that she should be remembered and not, as many so often insist on endorsing, as a cook or recipe writer. The clarity and style of Beeton's work is admirable, but she was not the innovator and culinary illuminati that Agnes was, or other peers that sit in her category, namely Eliza Acton, Constance Peel, or Eliza Warren Francis, who was one of the most established Victorian writers on the subject of household management.

Following the death of her first husband, Eliza took to writing and found she was both good at it and adept at gaining regular freelance work on the subject of sewing and general needlework. She delivered practical lessons on the subject and sustained a reasonable living, before remarrying and becoming a prolific authoress of books and magazine articles, branching out into household management and cookery. By 1849, she had become a 'celebrated Artiste in fancy Needlework', adding 'designer of patterns' to her repertoire. Her career progressed with rapidity on the death of her second husband, after which she successfully published a couple of books annually. Mrs Warren Francis became a household name in Britain and across the Atlantic. By 1857, she even had her own women's magazine, the *Ladies Treasury*, initially published by Ward and Lock, which remained popular for over twenty-five years. Undoubtedly Eliza would have been Isabella's biggest rival, with successful title after title including *Cookery for £200 a Year and for Great and Lesser Incomes*, *Cookery for All Incomes*, *A Series of Family Dinners and How to Carve Them*, and *Cookery Cards for the Kitchen*. Each one increased her celebrity status. Her friends included Sir Arthur Conan Doyle and the Rothschilds. Yet, unlike Mrs Beeton, the prolific work of Eliza Warren Francis remains largely forgotten.[1]

You will also discover in this book that Agnes Bertha Marshall may not have been the sole creator behind the Marshall brand and that her home life was not the rosy idyll one might have expected.

Her books, unlike Beeton's one masterpiece, are also somewhat dry and, I must admit, a tad pompous. If you like high-end French cuisine then Agnes is for you, otherwise you're hard pushed to find the few token simplistic recipes she threw in to keep the plebeians happy. She was, of course, the mistress of ices and for that I take my proverbial hat off to her.

Both Isabella and Agnes were working in and climbing the social ladder of a brave new world, one of mixed attitudes and contradictions, philanthropy and cruelty, early suffrage and misogyny, progress and poverty, literacy and child labour. I could go on. While the divide between rich and poor was being stop-gapped by the rising middle classes, poverty and disease were rife in Victorian society. It's as if Beeton and Marshall were balancing on the wheel of progress like so many others, both men and women wanting to make a difference, seeking acknowledgement and acceptance, and above all else being self-reliant, driven by aspiration and upward mobility.

To twenty-first century society with its labour-saving devices, advanced technology, and click convenience, Victorian-era work ethics appear almost other worldly. As a youth of the 1980s and 1990s, I remember starting work aged 13, labouring throughout all my holidays, evenings and many weekends as a student and then postgraduate student while studying, volunteering, and climbing my way up from the bottom of the pile, little by little. On reflection, this sometimes looks harsh even to me, but aspirational Victorians were largely doing it alone, self-funding; if they failed, they couldn't go and find another employer, they had to persevere and jolly well succeed. This is why many of their stories seem so big, even bigger when they are the stories of women, or people of different ethnicities, people with disabilities, because their struggles were so much more challenging. Saying that, we cannot disregard that Isabella and Agnes both had powerful, well-respected, and well-connected husbands to support them, although Isabella may not have had quite so much of that stability to rely on.

I chose to approach this book by focusing on both the lives and the works of our protagonists. Analysing their cookery books separately actually gave me further insight into their personalities, attitudes, and style. It also provided me with the scope to unpick and scrutinise some of the recipes individually.

I surprised myself writing this book and feel a sense of guilt towards my former attitude when it comes to Isabella Beeton. Sure, she didn't juggle a cookery school, write several books, invent, lecture, and innovate, but she was committed, passionate, and she faced greater hardships than Agnes. She made her mark more than any other female cookery writer, before or since. There is something about the no-nonsense tones of Isabella's writing and her practical best friend approach which remains appealing, comforting, and most importantly unpretentious.

While I will always most admire Agnes Bertha Marshall, I will never again compare the two unfavourably. Who knows, if Isabella had the wealth of Agnes and Alfred when they first embarked on their journey, or even if she had lived in the slightly more advanced world of the later Victorian era, she might have been the one who pioneered a cookery school or manufactured her own brands. If she had lived a bit longer, who knows what she could have been capable of. And this is the sad fact of many an enterprising young Victorians, who never got to reach their full potential, in an age when death was relentlessly at your door.

Chapter 1

Agnes Bertha Marshall

The Victorian and Edwardian eras are naturally the closest to us, in terms of what we might perceive as 'history'. Some of us still remember the stories shared by our grandparents about their parents (naming no names), who came from that generation. It is also a time that spawned huge amounts of media and written documentation, as the levels of literacy began to rise. In many ways, it is easier to interpret than something like the early medieval period where documentation is scant, often written in Latin or Old English, and biased to those in religious or political power. We can also relate more to the Victorian and Edwardian ages as they have been reproduced the most in literature and on screen; Charles Dickens, Thomas Hardy, Lewis Carroll, Arthur Conan Doyle, Oscar Wilde, H. G. Wells, and Bram Stoker all permeate our psyche with idealist Christmas pasts, feisty women, psychedelic tea parties, posh ladies who are easily insulted, time travel, and vampires, to name but a few.

It is a time which reflects the vast outpouring of talent, intellect, culture, the arts, and romanticism, all set against a conflicting background of social values, morality, religion, abject poverty, and economic change. The political system was slowly becoming more democratic in Britain, with voting extending beyond the confines of the privileged, but the decades of non-government intervention meant many individuals struggled in an unsupported economy. The Irish famine caused a vast wave of migrants, many of whom tried to establish themselves in English cities like Liverpool and London, cities that were already struggling with poverty, poor housing, and rising levels of disease. These weren't the only migrants. Britain's foreign policy was preoccupied with sustaining and increasing its overseas Empire. Although overseas immigration has a much longer legacy, Indian and African migrants who worked for the Navy or relocated to England found themselves trying to build a new life in the already overcrowded nineteenth-century port cities.

The class system was also changing to accommodate the rural masses settling into the urban growth of industry and technology, offering a cornucopia of employment opportunities. The aristocracy no longer had the monopoly on servants, fancy furniture, and fine cutlery. The Victorian age was largely built on the enterprising achievements of the middle classes. That said, it was the impoverished labouring classes who toiled in the dark, dangerous world of factories, mines, sewers, dockyards, and tunnels to both build and generate new industry.

At the height of Agnes's fame, cleaner water, improved drainage systems, new housing and imported cheaper goods, alongside labour-saving devices including gas and a sophisticated network of travel and transport systems, not to mention improvements in legislation for education and the poor, meant British society was steadily becoming more homogenous.

Photograph of Agnes Bertha Marshall circa 1880s/90s. Taken by the Queen's photographer W. & D. Downey. (Courtesy of Tony Haynes)

Early beginnings

> Gastronomy is not only a science in itself, but goes hand in hand with many other sciences, being almost inseparable from chemistry and physics, as well as commercial and political economy ... There can hardly be anything of greater importance to man than the knowledge of gastronomy. Everything that has life needs to be nourished and the character of our food affects our health, and through our health our minds.[1]

Although it would be a fall from a horse that ended Agnes Bertha Marshall née Smith's life in 1905, she had been suffering from synoptic, or lung cancer according to her death certificate.

The media collectively agreed that she was 'well known and loved'. Agnes was cremated at Golders Green Crematorium and interred in St John the Baptist churchyard, Pinner. The service was a large one attended by servants and outdoor staff from the Marshall family home, known as The Towers. The Pinner choir sang 'Oh God My Father, While I Stray', 'Now the Labourer's Task is Over' and 'Peace, Perfect Peace'. There was a procession

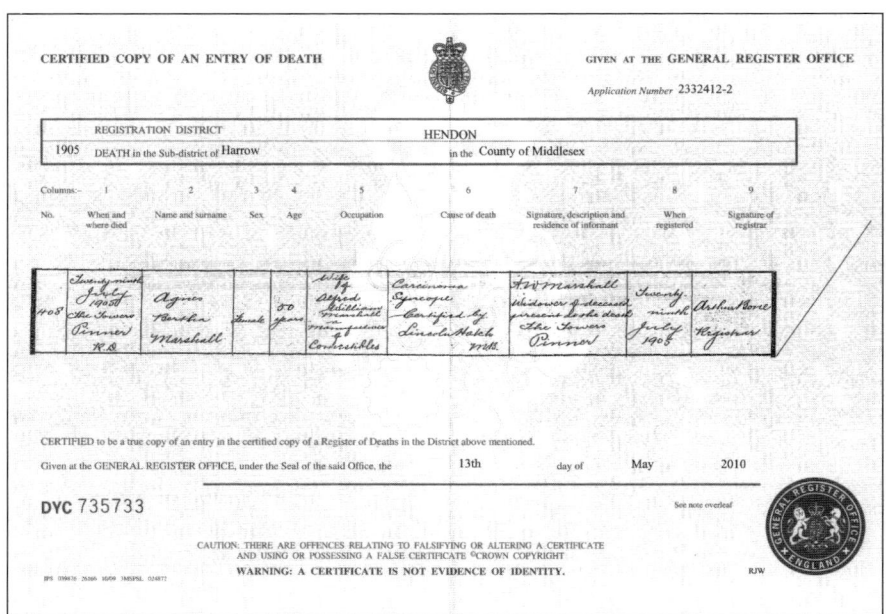

Death certificate of Agnes Bertha Marshall. (Courtesy of Tony Haynes)

John Salmon / *St John the Baptist, Church Lane, Pinner - East end* / CC BY-SA 2.0

through Pinner village and a peal rather than toll of bells, marking the end of this extraordinary woman's life.[2] A stained-glass window was even erected in her honour and can be seen at St John the Baptist's Church, Pinner.

It is undeniably clear from every newspaper report and written description of Agnes that she was a formidable culinary force and a gracious, methodical, organised worker. She was liked by everyone who came into contact with her and praised for her temperament and patience. What she was like as a mother and wife is less transparent. A great deal of thought was placed upon funeral hymns in the Victorian era. 'Oh God My Father While I Stray' is little known now, but was very popular at the time. As a hymn, it calls for an absolute commitment to God, allowing nothing to stand in the way of that devotion. It's very powerful and extremely devout, which is perhaps why it has become less popular in recent years and suggests Agnes was a passionate believer. 'Now the Labourer's Task is Over' also seems pertinent to a woman whose dedication to her work was infallible. The final hymn sung at Agnes's funeral symbolises an end to the trials of life and perhaps tranquillity after a time of suffering from the disease which consumed her. The fact that the church rang a peal of bells, opposed to a death knell, is also indicative of Agnes's high-status role in society.

In 1911, a fire destroyed significant records at the premises where the Marshall archives were stored at Ward, Lock & Co., Warwick House, London. The *Daily Telegraph & Courier* reported: 'Firemen and salvage men were at work all night, and throughout the day a mass of material representing hundreds and thousands of books was being shovelled from the upper storeys into the lane adjoining Warwick House, until that narrow cul de sac was piled many feet high with charred paper.'[3]

It has been suggested by some researchers that the fire that ravaged the Marshall archives may have taken place at Cassell's in 1955, as they were the new owners of Ward, Lock & Co. However, only part of the Ward Lock business was acquired by Cassell's and not until the 1980s. I would suggest the Marshall paperwork was therefore probably destroyed at Warwick House in 1911.

As a consequence, very little remains about the Marshall business activities, although it has been much speculated on over the years.

What we do know is that an Agnes Smith appears in the 1871 census living in a wealthy household, employed as a kitchen maid in a 'mansion house'. She is cited as being 18 years old, which would make her birth date around 1853, not 1855, which is often quoted as her date of birth, but dates were frequently distorted in the Victorian age. This Agnes was also born in Walthamstow, as was our Agnes. Could Agnes have begun her culinary journey as a kitchen maid? After all, we know very little about her background, status, or start in life. This is most probably conjecture, but considering information is scant and there is a connection, nothing can be ruled out. Alternatively, an Agnes Smith with a similar match can be found attending Bedford College, Bloomsbury, as a first-year student aged 14. Before it merged with Royal Holloway, it was a liberal ladies' college, founded and run by ladies. The learning on offer was pioneering, with subjects like science, maths, political economy, and Greek, as opposed to the etiquette lessons provided by most similar institutions of the day.

From an interview published in the *Pall Mall Gazette* in 1886, her husband Alfred Marshall was quoted as saying that 'Mrs Marshall I should tell you, has made a thorough study of cookery ever since she was a child, and has practised at Paris and Vienna under celebrated chefs.'[4] Agnes is also described as having trained in both Germany and France in an article in the *Cardiff Times*.[5]

Agnes's parents John and Susan Smith married in 1854, a year before Agnes was born, in Walthamstow. Nothing is known about John, except that he is named on Agnes's marriage certificate, referred to as a clerk. It's probable then that her early background was fairly lower middle class, considering her father's profession. Clerks were transcribers, mostly carrying out written tasks during a growing demand for administrative 'white collar workers' in a burgeoning industrial new world.

Was Agnes inspired by a family member to cook? We know from Alfred Marshall that she was familiar with it since childhood; if she was middle class, it must have been a humble household with few staff for her to become instructed in cookery, or perhaps, as suggested, she was employed in domestic work early on. She certainly seemed comfortable enough to employ her own half-sister Ada as her housekeeper.

There are absolutely no listings in the census for John, Susan, and their daughter Agnes. We do know, however, that her mother Susan was born in 1827/8 and probably died, relatively young, aged 56 in 1883.

We also know from other records listing her age that Agnes would have been born in or around 1855. According to the 1901 census, she was 44, which would actually make her birth date 1857 and her quoted age of 35 in 1891 would make her birthdate 1856.

As for Agnes's father John, it's as if he never existed and despite not being able to find any validation of the marriage itself, her mother Susan remarried John Wells, a cabinet maker from Cambridgeshire. They had three children together, three half-siblings to Agnes: Mary Sarah Wells (1859), John Osborne Wells (1864), and Ada Martha Wells (1868).

According to their marriage certificate, before she married Alfred in her early twenties, Agnes lived in Grafton Street, a fairly affluent part of London. In fact, it was the same street the famous actor Henry Irving occupied simultaneously and had once inhabited dukes, lords, earls, and MPs. We know that her mother and stepfather led a fairly comfortable life. But it was one without servants and trappings; they would not have been in a position to provide Agnes with the means to support herself independently. Is it possible that Agnes was working as a cook in the kitchens of a wealthy household on this street? Or perhaps she was offering tuition.

If she did travel far and wide to train as a culinary master, I can find no evidence of it in the passenger and travel lists. If she wasn't Agnes the kitchen maid, but the Agnes travelling Europe and learning to cook, this would legitimise her absence in census data, but it's confusing that there is no record of this. Agnes's training timeline would have preceded the boom in schools of culinary art, like the infamous Le Cordon Bleu, which didn't open until the 1890s. If part of her training was in Paris, it's likely Agnes would have been apprenticed to a pastry chef, caterer, or restaurant chef. Training could take around three years or more, it was intense and typically an all-male environment. Agnes may have learnt a different way of course, perhaps she paid for individual, private tuition, outside of the normal pastry shop/restaurant territory. If so, this suggests she hailed from a wealthy background. As her father was a humble clerk, it's doubtful he would have been able to invest in such a costly venture. Perhaps she had a wealthy benefactor, or perhaps she was headstrong and paid her own way.

Agnes may well have even worked as a cook in foreign kitchens. There was a big distinction between females as 'plain cooks' and men as chefs. By the end of the nineteenth century, thousands of French chefs were working in London alone, but no French women, as far as I know. There are some accounts of female-led kitchens in France during the 1890s, most notably the Hotel Foyet, Paris, where the *Illustrated London News* of 13 June 1891 informs us: 'In the vast kitchens, where a small army of cooks and scullions had laboured to prepare the banquets of their masters, a single female chef, assisted by three maids, toiled daily to supply the limited pensionnaires of the establishment with their morning and evening meals.' In Bilhères, Southwest France, a restaurant called the Clubhouse, according to the *Field* newspaper of 17 January 1891, was run by 'a most meritorious female chef' where the food was 'excellent'. One of the very first renowned female French chefs was Eugenie, or 'Mere' Brazier and that wasn't until the first quarter of the twentieth century. It's true to say that the statistics relating to the status of professional female chefs working in country estates, restaurants, or hotels in nineteenth-century Europe is extremely scarce. Even more so in England. The *Forres*

Elgin and Nairn Gazette, Northern Review and Advertiser published a particularly pertinent article on 29 May 1867:

> Let us take cookery, my friends. It is one of the common employments of women. Essentially, cookery is a rational art. There is reason, you know, in roasting an egg. Now many women are good executive cooks. But if you want a head-cook you must resort to the stronger sex. There are female mathematicians – they are very few; but perhaps a female mathematician is less rare than a female chef. Who are the cooks that invent the great dishes? Not women, I think. Where is your female Ude? Where is your female Soyer? A lady once stated that she had made some mock turtle out of her own head. She not only made a dish, but a joke. She was one of the exceptions. Request one of the gentler sex, my friends to boil you a round of beef, for instance, after the manner prescribed by Liebig. With an amiable docility, which cannot be extolled too highly, she will perhaps obey you, but try to make her apprehend the principle of the process ? No, don't – if you persist in the endeavour she will probably cry, and the man who would drew a tear does the cheek of loveliness by useless explanation or argument is no better than a Bluebeard.
>
> I said, my friends, that there are exceptions to the generality of women: I took care to say so. There are some women undeniably endowed with reason. You may never have met with such: I will not enumerate or name them: how few they may be no matter. The fact of their existence is consolatory. It enables us to believe that the genius, at least, of reason exists in the mind of every woman, and that, in the great mass of women that divine faculty is only dormant.

I'm not sure where to start with unpicking this assault on the character of women. A passive-aggressive and prejudiced tirade which perfectly illustrates the attitudes of the time. Women were simply not quick-witted enough to solve the complicated technical machinations of real cookery. Neither were they even allowed to try. Perhaps this is why Agnes was so consumed by creating, extolling, and teaching haute cuisine. Yes, it was fashionably integral to society, but she also had a lot to prove as someone with a 'dormant' intellect.

Germany in the 1800s was an up-and-coming powerhouse of central Europe, growing as a strong competitor to French cuisine. Alfred Marshall mentions nearby Vienna as another location where Agnes trained. The references to female chefs employed as both caterers and hotel restaurant kitchen staff are numerous in Germany as the nineteenth century tipped over into the next. The royal kitchens of Austria were well documented as superior to those of Queen Victoria's and according to the 1894 periodical, *Current Opinion*, despite being headed up by men, many of the kitchen apprentice chefs, bakers, and 'coffee women' were female.

Agnes may well have received more cosmopolitan instruction on the continent, as well as gaining a greater understanding of European cuisine and cooking, considering the slight differentiation in earlier attitudes to female culinarians.

Agnes had clearly flown the nest before marrying, if there had ever been a nest to fly from, as her mother and stepfather were busy raising their own new family without Agnes, in the sprawling industrial London suburb of Haggerston, now in Hackney, in the 1870s. Agnes's stepfather, John Wells, came from a long line of cabinet makers, a skill which was predominantly middle class. The main manufacturing districts in London during the nineteenth century included Shoreditch, where the Wells family lived for some ten years, and Hackney, their last listed residence. So John worked in the very heart of his trade, probably making a range of furniture, from beautiful inlaid cabinets to mass-produced bedroom suites. By the end of the century, he may have struggled as consumerism and the demand for cheap furniture forced the bespoke trade into decline.

In 1881, Susan and John Wells, their son John, and daughter Ada lived together at 132 Blurton Road, Hackney, London, a nice but fairly standard terraced four-bedroom house in East London. Also living at that address was Agnes's first child, Ethel. Ethel's surname is given as Smith, not Marshall. Was the marriage of Agnes and Alfred a shotgun wedding? Or was Ethel the child of someone else, with Alfred marrying Agnes to maintain her reputation? The Civil Registration of her birth in 1878 (between April and June) lists her as Ethel Doyle Smith, not

Marshall, while Agnes married Alfred later in August that same year. The application of Agnes's maiden name may of course be due to the fact that Ethel was not yet baptised, although the dates are certainly irregular. Children conceived out of 'sin' were not only rejected by society, but they also symbolised immorality, as the fruits conceived of their fornicating parents. People believed these immoralities were transferred directly to the child. It was common to force a daughter to leave her home if she became pregnant without being married. She would either need to start a life on her own with her illegitimate child as far away from the family as possible, or farm the child out to a specialist baby murderer for a set fee (yes, that was actually a profession). The other option was the workhouse and many may have pleaded for death before submitting to that. Premarital pregnancies were rare among the middle classes. For a start, they were chaperoned everywhere and taught above all else to suppress urges. Marriage would have been inevitable for Agnes, considering her situation.

Alfred and Agnes were living in a substantial property in London at the time of the 1881 census, with their one-year-old daughter Agnes Alfreda and newborn son Alfred Marshall; it's not as if they didn't have the means to care for Ethel. Perhaps three children all under the age of three was too much for Agnes to look after and she called on her mother for support. This was common practice.

Although the Wells family was fairly large (even more so with a young granddaughter to care for), they didn't employ servants, which probably meant they were not that financially comfortable. From the records, it seems likely that both Susan and John were dead by their late fifties or early sixties.

Their daughter Mary Sarah Wells was the oldest known half-sister of Agnes, supposedly born around 1859, just a few years after Agnes, in the wake of the disappearance or death of the elusive John Smith. Sometime during the early part of the twentieth century, Mary moved to Ontario, Canada, with her husband Robert Wacey and three of their seven children, touchingly, one named Agnes. Had Mary and her half-sister been close? Her early married life must have been quite difficult, both with working-class professions, living in an overly built-up urban district of London, then relocating and moving around Birmingham, possibly for Robert's work as a glass silverer. Perhaps they moved to Canada for a better standard of life. Hundreds of thousands of British and Irish citizens left their own shores for those of Canada throughout the nineteenth century to seek work and escape the ever-increasing population, which impacted on the labour market and the economy generally. This wave of escapism and the pull of the New World, with its wide-open spaces, promises of wealth, opportunity, and less challenging circumstances made places like the United States, Canada, and Australia very appealing options for young workers and families.

Whatever new life Mary and Robert made for themselves, it was enough to keep them and their children in Canada for the rest of their lives.

By 1901, Agnes's half-brother John Osborne Wells, then in his mid-thirties, was married to Catherine Fanny Waterman and they lived in salubrious Redcliffe Road, Chelsea, a far cry from his birthplace of Kingsland, a poor and densely populated area of London near Dalston. He had obviously gained Agnes's confidence, being entrusted to manage Marshall's stores and cookery school, a position he continued to hold ten years later. Considering his previous jobs included messenger and clerk, John must have been delighted with his change of circumstances. It appears that Catherine never worked or had to work and the couple had no children.

The youngest Wells daughter was Ada Martha and sadly hers was a short life. After a brief stint as Agnes's housekeeper, at just 24 she, like her older sister, emigrated, this time to South Africa, where she married, but died giving birth to her daughter, Kathleen Lilian Agnes. Ada's husband was from Liverpool and seems to have had a colourful and adventurous life as a cook at sea and a bookmaker's assistant before becoming a journalist of renown with quite a reputation. Thomas McDonald founded two newspapers in South Africa, the *Zoutpansberg Review* and the *Beira Post* (1898). He sailed to America in 1876, moving to South Africa the following year, where he fought in the Zulu wars and prospected for gold before establishing himself as a journalist.

Ada travelled as an unmarried woman from Southampton to South Africa, which for a 24-year-old in 1892 was quite plucky and fiercely independent, although it was also likely that both her parents were dead by this time and Ada may have been seeking financial security and a more prosperous future. Interestingly, her occupation on the passenger list is that of cook.

Whether the experience of working for her half-sister Agnes was so harrowing that it drove Ada to leave the country, she had a restless spirit, or was following a lover out there is something we will never know. Neither will we know if Agnes was close to her half-siblings.

Given Mary named a daughter after her, John was entrusted to run her business, and Ada was employed as her housekeeper, perhaps even inspired to cook by her sister, it's likely they were fond of each other. Ada also bestowed the middle name Agnes to her daughter. It would appear there was a genuine connection between all four of Susan's children.

Family and home

Although an average lifetime is pitted with both joy and sadness, an overwhelming gloominess pervaded the lives of all Agnes's children, including abandonment, a tragic death, eternal spinsterhood, separation, bankruptcy, apathy, and only one grandchild.

In 1878, Agnes married Alfred William Marshall at St George's Church, Hanover Square, London. She would have been in her early twenties. Although we know nothing of their courtship, we do know that Agnes was pregnant before they got hitched.

While Ethel Doyle Marshall's very early years were spent with her grandparents, she also attended an independent and very exclusive girls' school in Brighton, together with her sister, Agnes junior. At 13 Arundel Terrace, Brighton, was a school for young girls aged 11 to 18. Here, no more than ten pupils were instructed in, among other things, English, French, and German. Built in the Regency era, Arundel Terrace, consisting of thirteen stunning houses facing the sea, complete with Doric porches and wrought-iron balconies, remains a striking feature of Brighton's landscape. Formerly a hotel, Ethel and Agnes's school has now been converted into apartments, as have most of the other terraced properties, although they were once populated by famous novelists, painters, war heroes, journalists, and actors. Agnes's daughters studied in luxurious ten-bedroom surroundings, with a drawing room, dining room, library, kitchen, separate servants' quarters, outdoor space, and even water closets (bathrooms).[6] It's not

St George's Church, Hanover Square, where Alfred and Agnes were married.

Marriage Certificate of Agnes and Alfred. (Courtesy of Tony Haynes)

clear whether Agnes and Ethel boarded at the school, but their absence from home would suggest they did.

Brighton held the nickname 'School Town' in the nineteenth century as dozens of elite private schools were established in the area, the famous Roedean being one of them. Roedean was also for girls aged 11–18. This school would probably have been beyond the means of Agnes and Alfred, despite the couple's growing status. It also prepared girls specifically for university during a time when women's education was becoming more accessible and intrinsic to society. Had Agnes wanted her girls to progress to higher education and a career, or had she simply wanted to prepare them for conventional society? She was, after all, a dynamic entrepreneur and businesswoman herself. Some of the latest research on entrepreneurship in Victorian Britain, according to economic historian Carry van Lieshout, reveals that almost 30 per cent of businesses were being run by women between 1851 and 1911 and these businesses varied from grocers, to teachers, farming, and lodging house keepers to name a few. There is also a strong correlation between marital status and the type of businesses these women ran. Dressmakers and teachers, for example, were the least inclined to get married, while farming women were often widowed. In fact, only laundresses and grocers were likely to be married.

Agnes and Alfred ran their business venture together and it was a unique enterprise in many ways, so less likely to be a statistic, but for those women like Agnes, choosing to remain in the workforce after childbirth, as opposed to having no choice, life would indeed have been much more rewarding and enriching. Many people are often surprised to learn that historically women, despite their lack of equality in society, were economically prosperous. During the century before Agnes's own enterprises, significant numbers of women worked in trade and manufacturing in the larger cities as business owners in their own right, from supplying candles to the aristocracy, to haberdashers and hat makers. It is definitely an aspect of history which is often overlooked. While we are likely to gasp in wonderment at women like Agnes battling it out in the eighteenth century, it's important to recognise that there were and had been many other female entrepreneurs with far more demanding jobs and lifestyles to contend with, most of which are confined to the archives.

What Agnes's daughter Ethel Marshall did after leaving school in Brighton around 1896 is inconclusive, but by 1900, she was married to Albert Neve Newman and she had been living with her family in Pinner at The Towers. The media widely reported on the marriage. Albert was from Ludlow and the couple were married at St Mary's, Bryanston Square, London. Alfred gave her away. It was undoubtedly a swanky affair, with a full choral service, which was 'largely attended'. A reception followed at the Hotel Great Central (now the Landmark, London) with some 200 guests. The couple honeymooned in Paris. Ethel gave Albert a silver travelling bag as a gift and in return he gave his new wife a silver dressing bag. Agnes and Alfred gifted the couple a silver chest, table cutlery, household linen, a drawing room clock, a 'centre-piece', and Dresden vases. Her brothers gifted her fish knives and forks and her sister a salad bowl. Her uncle John O. Wells gave Dresden china fruit dishes. Among other trinkets, Albert Neve Newman's employees contributed a china dinner service and paid for 'outdoor servants' and 'indoor servants' for them to utilise at The Towers. It's a little shocking in a way to thinks of servants being gifted as presents. Alfred's employees gave silver scent bottles, while the bridegroom's parents handed over a silver cruet set and a cheque (I'd loved to have known how much for). The list of items goes on and on.[7]

This wedding seems to have been a lavish statement of wealth more than anything else, with Alfred and Agnes at the height of their careers, revelling in London society. The reality for Albert and Ethel, however, was beginning their married lives slightly beyond their means, in illustrious Holland Park Gardens, Kensington. A life that would cruelly take its revenge when just four years later, Albert was facing bankruptcy and claiming ill health, which left him unable to run the branches of his London mantle and costumiers.[8] He died aged just 38 that same year.

Interior of Great Central Hotel, Winter Gardens, Ethel and Albert's wedding reception venue.

Ethel lived a much longer life, dying at her home 74 Onslow Gardens, Kensington, London in 1961.[9] Judging by the neighbourhood, she did not die in poverty. She didn't marry again and after Albert died, she resided in a rather upmarket boarding house in Paddington, funding herself by 'private means' along with eight other boarders and three servants to take care of them. Ethel's profession is listed as a cook, living in Camberwell in 1939.[10]

Could she have been working at Marshall's? Despite being the youngest of Agnes's children, Ethel lived into her eighties, outliving all her family apart from her much younger half-sister Rosalie, to whom she bequeathed her estate of £4,467.[11]

Had Agnes's eldest child Ethel no one else to bestow her assets upon, or had she a good relationship with her half-sister? Over the course of just four years, Ethel lost her husband, her mother, and her brother. It must have been extraordinarily tough. I wonder if she became a little reclusive.

Like her sister, Agnes Alfreda moved back to Pinner and her parents' home sometime after her education. There is little information relating to Agnes junior, aside from some records of a bankruptcy order being filed against her in 1924 listing her address at the time as 1 Ranelagh Grove, Ebury Bridge, London. She is also registered a spinster, aged 45.[12] Her only nephew Noel was living with her a few years before she died at 5 Laverton Place, together with someone called Annie Lambe, who may have been a domestic servant. By the time of her death, her address was 32 Mortimer Street, on the site of Marshall's Cookery School. This implies that Agnes Alfreda may have been working at Marshall's during its final years trading. She actually died age 54 at St Mary Abbots Hospital which was an infirmary and workhouse, closed in the 1990s, before being demolished and replaced by housing. In 1935, when Agnes died, Abbotts had become a hospital for patients with chronic illnesses. She left over £1,000 to her brother William Edward Marshall, a sizeable sum equivalent to about £50,000 today. William was registered as a Company Director at this time.[13]

Nothing was bequeathed to Agnes's sister Ethel. Perhaps the money was intended to fund the ailing cookery school. There is a note on Agnes's register of burials, instructing cremation. There was no minister at her service.[14]

Agnes and Alfred must have had high hopes for their first son Alfred Harold, once described as 'a clever draftsman'. But the young, privileged Alfred junior, educated privately in Brighton and at Rugby School before being apprenticed into a well-known engineering company, had his character very publicly scrutinised during a court case in 1904. An indignant Alfred senior was incensed by accusations made about his son's tardiness and defiance and went after the man who terminated Alfred junior's apprenticeship, John Henry Lock. The court case was savage, with Lock criticising many aspects of Alfred Harold's character, traits which he believed let his genuine talent down. At one stage, John Lock even insinuated that Alfred senior and his family were to blame. Some of these criticisms included a daily routine of starting work at 11.30 am then leaving at 1.00 pm for dinner (lunch) and not returning until 4.00 before vacating the premises at 5.00. Agnes and Alfred's son also allegedly refused to wear a cap at work. Alfred senior reclaimed any losses incurred from the funds he'd contributed towards his son's apprenticeship, but the Marshalls' reputation had been more than a little scarred.[15]

Was this the problem with the Marshall children, did their advantages in life make them unmotivated? The extent to which parental absenteeism and neglect played a part in their young lives while Agnes and Alfred forged ahead with their careers must also have contributed to a general sense of despondency. Whatever Alfred Harold's issues were with authority and punctuality, he would never have an opportunity to rectify them, as four years after his failed apprenticeship, he died in 1908 of consumption aged just 27. Having been seriously ill for over two years, Alfred Harold Marshall finally died at the Home Sanitorium in Bournemouth, Dorset, where he had resided for some time to aid his recuperation. He was cremated in Golders Green and laid to rest in the family vault with his mother in Pinner Cemetery.[16]

The youngest and possibly the most successful of all Agnes and Alfred's children was William Edward Marshall. He too almost met with an untimely death, involved in a near-fatal motorcycle accident one Sunday in September 1904, when he was motoring between Harrow and Pinner. He did, however, receive head injuries. William inherited Alfred's passion for the voluntary fire brigade, becoming captain of the local Pinner branch, just as his father before him had.[17]

He married Katherine Josephine Marshall in 1903 and the couple appeared to be living well, with neither of them listed as having occupations in Northumberland Mansions, Marylebone. They had one son, Noel Claude Marshall, born in 1909, who went on to become a French language interpreter and was decorated as major in the Second World War. Noel was the sole benefactor of his father's will of around £5,000 in 1951, worth over £150,000 in today's purchasing power.

'Company Director' William Edward Marshall was involved in a scandal in 1935, resulting in the death of his mistress Betty Houghton. Betty had lived at resplendent 37 Connaught Street, Paddington as William's mistress since around 1928. It was a volatile relationship, particularly as Betty had a serious drinking problem and a history of mental illness, culminating in an incident leading to a fatal head injury. A witness claimed William Edward Marshal and Alfred's youngest son had never hurt his partner, despite her ongoing abusive behaviour, and there was significant evidence to suggest it was an accidental death.[18] The trial for this case is painful to read, a high-profile, active businessman entangled in a toxic relationship with a woman who had undergone treatment for years, with no other form of income, completely unstable, who regularly succumbed to emotional blackmail and abuse in order to obtain money for alcohol and socialising. Witnesses including doctors and domestic staff claimed William was tolerant and unresponsive to any violence in her company, despite regular verbal arguments over her spending habits.

By 1939, William was living alone in a flat in Westbourne St, Paddington, listed as a 'Company Director'. In fact, Agnes and Alfred's son had become managing director of Marshall's School of Cookery, a role he had been active in since at least 1913.[19] Despite living alone, he is also cited as being married, so he and Katherine most likely separated rather than divorced. William Edward died at home aged 69. Like his sister Agnes, he was cremated and no minister presided at the ceremony.

There is evidence to suggest that a William Edward Marshall was estranged from his wife, while living in Paddington between at least 1928 until his death in 1939, perhaps spending much of his time in a dysfunctional relationship with a woman whose death he may have been involved in, his alibi a game of golf. His wife Katherine is more difficult to follow. She died listed as a widow in 1960, further confirmation that she and William never divorced. Her final place of residence was a small village in Essex and her will totalled a paltry £299, which she bequeathed to her son Noel.

Had William Edward Marshall always been an adulterer? If so, why choose to be with a woman who would undoubtedly have made his life miserable? Unless it was a controlling relationship on his part, which would make Agnes and Alfred's son a rather unpleasant sort of man. He did endure a head injury in early life – did this impact on his behaviour, or was he more of an emotionally broken individual, losing his mother at a young age, swiftly followed by his brother, watching his father remarry almost immediately and growing up in a household with absent career parents, provided with every convenience and opportunity his upbringing gave him? Such circumstances could have made William Edward vulnerable and emotionally dependent in a relationship. He may have wanted to rescue Betty Houghton, but ultimately failed, as so many do in those unfortunate situations. It's frustrating to come to terms with the fact that we will never really know. One thing is certain, however; the Marshall children were an unusual clan of misfits, slightly tragic and flawed figures which may have been a consequence of their upbringing or genetic identity. Agnes's only grandchild, Noel, seemingly ended the line of that branch of Marshalls. Although he is registered as being married in 1939, he was living alone in Hampstead. There is a possibility that Noel married someone called Sylvia Morton in 1932, but if he did, they were estranged.

At home

Despite buying The Towers, a sprawling old property with acres of land in Pinner, some six years earlier, according to the 1891 census Agnes and Alfred were actually living across 30 and 32 Mortimer Street, the premises of the cookery school, together with eight servants including Agnes's half-sister Ada, who they employed as their housekeeper. Agnes Alfreda would have utilised this same living space later in life when she also resided at the property. Perhaps they were still renovating The Towers at this time, or were working so intensely at the school that it made more sense to live there temporarily. I wonder if the Marshalls may not always have kept their own staff happily employed, when it was reported in 1897 that their cook of some five years, Bridget Gilhooly, had stolen tablecloths, forks, antimacassars, and other property which she then passed onto a local publican, a man also formerly employed by the Marshalls.[20]

From the transcript of the trial notes for this case, we actually get to hear the voices of Alfred and Agnes directly, giving us a sense of their physical selves, both ragingly determined to seek justice for their stolen belongings, going as far as to sit in vigil for hours at the accused's house. I can't stop wondering, when reading about the case, how they could have managed the situation differently. The act of theft was clearly one of desperation and for all those involved, it seemed their former staff had far much more to lose than the Marshalls. Many working-class people lived on the breadline in Victorian London and small thefts from employees were undoubtedly rife. It doesn't make it acceptable, but both Bridget and the Marshalls' former porter appear to have been of good character. Giving thought to this whole incident, it seems questionable as to why Agnes and Alfred didn't just terminate Bridget's employment, rather than pursue the incident with such righteousness. Perhaps this is why, unusually, despite all the evidence against the Marshalls' staff, they were ultimately found not guilty.

> ALFRED WILLIAM MARSHALL. I live at the Towers, at Pinner – my wife and I have a business in Mortimer Street – a woman named Bridget Gilhooly was in our service as cook for some time – the prisoner was also in our service, as a porter and odd man in the business in 1885 – recently he has been, I believe, manager of a public-house in Farringdon Street – I have not seen him there – in our house at Pinner we had a quantity of linen and other articles – on January 11th Bridget Gilhooly went for a holiday – she did not come back that night – next day, in consequence of inquiries, I sent for the police, and they were at the house when Gilhooly returned – after some time her boxes were searched, and in them were found some fifty articles, which I recognised, which should not have been in her possession, linen, and other things – I gave her into custody, and she was taken

away by the police – in her box was found a letter – on January 13th I went to the Sportsman public-house in Great Saffron Hill, where the prisoner was employed – I had sworn an information for a search warrant – a police inspector and two officers went with me and my wife, and the house was searched, and three table-covers, six linen tablecloths, two pillow slips, and two pairs of cuffs, these were found in various parts of the premises – I identified them as my property – they were of the value of £5 – some of the articles had my mark on them – these two pillows were on the bed, which I presume was the bed slept in by the prisoner – the mark on them has been cut out – this pillow slip has also had the name cut out – I recognise these two table-covers – one of them is quite new – it is a special size, and had been specially ordered – the mark on the tape has been removed – after waiting some time the prisoner came home – after the search I remained with the officer – when the prisoner came in he asked Mrs. Marshall, 'Have you lost anything?' – she said, 'Yes, a great many, Patrick' – the officer asked him to open a cupboard which was in the corner of the room – he produced the key; the cupboard was undone; the officers began searching it – the prisoner walked up and down the room, passing jeering remarks, such as 'This is lovely' – I think he was sober – he said, 'Let Mr. Marshall look in there himself; don't push the things about; he won't find anything there' – then Mr. Weller put these things on the table in a brown paper parcel, and said, 'What about these things?' and when the prisoner saw them he said, 'I am don?' – the initials on it are our family initials – the officer told him he would be charged with stealing them – he said, 'I am a ruined ma?' – he asked the boy in the bar for brandy, which he had, and he offered the officers something to drink, which they did not have; he was taken away – he was afterwards before the Justices with Gilhooly, and he was committed for trial.

Cross-examined. The prisoner was in our service something under two years – he left with a good character in December,

1885 – he then went to the Aquarium, and then into the London police – this is the first time that any accusation has been made against him – Mrs. Marshall and I went to the Sportsman about half-past seven; we waited outside about half an hour with Inspector Weller, and two other officers – we went inside about eight, and remained there till one, when the prisoner came in – besides the prisoner, I saw Mary Gilhooly in the house – she is the sister of Bridget Gilhooly – Mary is the licensee of the house – the boy was employed there as potman or barman – there was no barmaid – they were in the house when we got there – Miss Gilhooly was serving behind the bar – before the prisoner came in, I and the officers had gone into every room in the house and searched, and the linen in question was produced – there was a room upstairs which we had not seen, because the prisoner had the key – I have no recollection who opened that door – these cuffs were among the linen produced; I don't think they have been washed – they have ragged edges; it is not a clean cut – I had a solicitor at the Court before the Magistrate – I did not mention to the Magistrate that the prisoner said, 'I am done'; I was not asked the question; I told it to my solicitor – I know now that the prisoner lived at Kensal Rise, and that he holds an occasional spirit licence there – I thought he was fully licensed for athletic sports – I know that my wife has been in the habit of giving away old articles of clothing.

Re-examined. These cuffs are new – the pillow slips were marked in a particular place, where the tears are now.

AGNES BERTHA MARSHALL. I am the wife of the last witness, living at Pinner – I recognise the articles produced; they are our property – I never give away household linen – I keep a school of cookery in Mortimer Street, and for that purpose use old linen.

WALTER WELLER. I am a police inspector, stationed at Pinner – on January 13th I received a search warrant granted by the Magistrates, and went, with Mr. and Mrs. Marshall and two officers, to the Sportsman public-house, on Saffron Hill – I made a search of the house, and found the articles produced in the front parlour downstairs; the three table-cloths were in the wash house; the three table-covers were in a bedroom upstairs, where the prisoner sleeps – the pillow slips were on the bed, and the collars were in the same room – Mr. Marshall said they were his property – with the exception of these articles there was no other linen in the house – we waited in the house till the prisoner came home, about one in the morning – I told him we were police officers, and said, 'Have you received any property from Mrs. Gilhooly at the Towers, Pinner?' – he said, 'No' – I said, 'We have a search warrant, and have searched your house' – at the same time I picked up these articles, and put them on the table, and said, 'These things have been found, and identified by Mr. Marshall, and you will be charged with receiving them, knowing them to be stolen' – as I showed him some of the articles he said, 'I am a ruined man; this takes the cake' – I made a note of what he said the same day – I think that was all he said.

Cross-examined. I got an address, 'Victor Road, Kensal Rise' – it was occupied by the prisoner – after he was in custody, I went there and searched the house – I found no stolen articles there – I saw his two children there; his wife was out; there was another woman in the house – I believe his wife and children live there; that is some miles from Saffron Hill – I have not made inquiries about the prisoner – he is known – nothing is known against him – he was once in the police, and afterwards held situations in public-houses – he was in the habit of applying to the Magistrate for an occasional licence – of course, a man who holds a licence must be of good character.

Re-examined. When we first went into the Sportsman a young woman and a boy were there; they did not leave the house while I was there – no message was sent to the prisoner while

I was there – he came in with a latch-key; we heard him open the door; I did not see anyone with him – he came there to stay till the morning.

MRS. MARSHALL (*Re-called*). When the prisoner came in he looked and seemed very astonished to see us there – when Inspector Weller said he was a detective, and held a search warrant, he walked up and down the room, and, looking at the things, said, 'This is lovely; this takes the cake;' and so on – when the linen was placed on the table, he said, 'Oh, I am done' – I believe that was the phrase – he afterwards said he was a ruined man.

Cross-examined. I did not go with my husband to Mr. Box, the solicitor, to have my proof taken – I did not make a note of the conversation.

Re-examined. I told Mr. Marshall that I remembered what the prisoner said.

INSPECTOR WELLER (*Re-examined*). I have my note, and have read it through – what the prisoner said was, 'I am a ruined man' – I do not remember his saying anything else – there were two more bedrooms upstairs; there was not much clothing in them – there was a little bed in one of them; one of the rooms was occupied by the barman, and the other by Miss Gilhooly – the other was a bedroom apparently occupied by someone.

NOT GUILTY.[21]

The Marshalls' beloved property, The Towers, which was first put up for auction in 1882, was formerly known as Temple Farm and it was situated in Pinner, an affluent suburb of London. The property was on the market for several years before Agnes and Alfred bought and converted it in 1885. Today, all that remains of the site resides under what is now called Lloyd Court, a housing estate built in the 1960s. The Towers was a five-minute walk from the new London Underground station on the Metropolitan line, which opened in 1885 and would have made the commute into the city an easy one for the busy Marshalls. But the station also opened the area up to less wealthy people, which led to the modernisation and mass development of Pinner. In the mid-1800s, this charming former medieval hamlet was attracting aspirational couples and families with its fashionable location and growing community. Pinner is the birthplace of many notable celebrities including Elton John and coincidentally was home to Samuel and Isabella Beeton.

An article in the *Harrow Observer*, 1910, best describes The Towers:

> A beautiful, old-fashioned house, well back from the road, and is approached by two carriage drives. There are twelve bed and dressing rooms, two bathrooms, hall, two reception and a full-sized billiard room, winter garden and conservatory, capital offices, including servants' hall, annexe, consisting of a school room, three bachelors' bedrooms, stabling for seven horses, entrance lodge, coachman's quarters; laundry engine house; beautiful pleasure grounds, through which flows the river Pin; wide spreading lawns, tennis pavilion, flower garden, rose and shrubbery walks, lily pond, fruit and vegetable garden and glass houses over 7 and a half acres.[22]

Pinner Local History Society recalls 'The Towers was an imposing dwelling at the corner of West End Lane and Eastcote Road; the house had a couple of little turrets which gave it its name, one of them containing a chiming clock.'[23]

Two photographs exist of the outside of the property showing either Agnes or one of her daughters in the driving seat of a car, probably the earlier image of the two, and a wonderful family picture all seated together in another car. The latter, as far as I know, is the only photograph of the family. Possibly Alfred Harold is driving, or his brother William, Alfred senior next to him, while Agnes sits directly behind William with Agnes Alfreda and Ethel on the end. The chap languishing in the doorway may well be their butler, Franz Schuler. I would like to hazard a guess that this photograph was taken some time between 1900 and 1905. All the children would have been in their early twenties. Considering the first car to be built in Britain was 1895, with commercial car manufacturing not active until at least 1901, the Marshalls' vehicle would have been uncommon and costly.

Agnes or one of her daughters in a motor car outside The Towers.

Marshall family in their motor car, outside The Towers.

The photographs depict The Towers as a charming old house which has been fashioned in the Arts and Crafts style of the time, beautiful brickwork which undoubtedly would have been red, veiled in ivy. Gabled windows and an impressive arched entrance give the effect of grandeur and wealth, an image Agnes and Alfred were keen to display – self-made, entrepreneurial, and successful.

The Towers was clearly a luxury residence, a place for Agnes and her family to enjoy country pursuits and much-needed leisure time. For Agnes, in her spare moments there was nothing more rewarding than hosting friends at The Towers with its bright flowers, homely atmosphere and numerous pets.[24]

In 1901, the Marshalls employed the following staff:

- Anna Vogel, housekeeper, aged 34, German
- Eliza Watts, cook, aged 39
- Alma Franceschi, housemaid, aged 24, Austrian
- Ada Carpenter, scullery maid, aged 14
- Anna Cock, housemaid, aged 26, German
- Franz Schuler, butler, aged 27, German

Interestingly, Agnes listed herself as a commercial farmer at the property's original name of Temple Farm in the Kelly's Directory of 1898. The seven acres of land may have been partly agricultural. We know there was a vegetable garden and hot houses; perhaps this land provided the cookery school with its ingredients and for developing the many branches of grocery items Agnes and Alfred manufactured.

By 1908, Alfred and his new wife Gertrude had set up residence in London. There was also a small piece that appeared in the *Harrow Observer* in 1910 detailing the sale of The Towers, bought at auction for £7,500. This sale must not have been finalised as there is plenty of evidence to suggest the Marshalls were still very much the owners as late as 1914 when they opened up their gardens to local residents. Some 500 people accepted the invitation to walk among the flowerbeds, roses, lily ponds, and sprawling lawns. Alfred and Gertrude entertained the crowd with a 'gramophone concert'.

That same year, The Towers' extensive tennis courts played host to the finals of the West End Lawn Tennis Club where Gertrude handed out the prizes together with her daughter Rosalie.[25]

Original tin of Mrs Marshall's portable jellies and blancmanges. (© Emma Kay)

Alfred William Marshall

In 1879, just one year after marrying Agnes, Alfred was sentenced at the Central Criminal Court, London to six months in Holloway prison for embezzlement. The story of the trial was covered by the media:

> ALLEGED FRAUDS BY A PARTNER. At the Central Criminal Court, Alfred William Marshall, 31, a gentlemanly-looking man, described a member of firm of wine merchants,

has been indicted with embezzling and stealing two bankers' cheques for £100 each, and one for £74 16s. 6d., the property of the said co-partnership. Mr. Besley conducted the prosecution, and Mr. Montagu Williams appeared for the defendant. The case appeared to be out- of a rather complicated character, but it seemed from the opening statement of the learned counsel for the prosecution that the prosecutor was a gentleman named Crusoe, who is engaged in the same trade at Xeres, in Spain, and that he had entered into partnership with the prisoner for the purpose of carrying on the wine trade this country, ana premises at 10 and 11, Mincing-lane, were engaged for the purpose, the arrangement being that the wines should transmitted to this country by the prosecutor, and that the prisoner should have the entire management of the business in London, under certain restrictions, and the profits, if any, were to be divided between them. It was on the part of the prosecution that the defendant had misappropriated certain monies that had come into his hands, and also that he had improperly obtained money by depositing wines as security, concealing the fact from the prosecutor, and afterwards appropriated the money to his own use.[26]

This act of embezzlement suggests another side to Alfred, a side that had the capacity to break the law and to deceive. The fact that he may also have compromised Agnes's honour by sleeping with her prior to marriage, resulting in pregnancy (a heinous crime back in the nineteenth century) is perhaps characteristic of Alfred's less attractive qualities.

Originally trained as a tutor, Buckinghamshire-born Alfred came from a socially aspiring family who provided him with a private education, eventually leading to a promising position of assistant master at a boys' school in Reading. Alfred chose a solo career delivering private tuition, working in London, before re-styling himself as a 'merchant', 'manufacturer of culinary requisites', and finally a 'gelatine merchant'.

More information about the Marshall patented freezer and ice cave can be found in the following chapter and there has always been an assumption that Agnes was the one who invented these innovative gadgets, while concocting the various food dyes and other culinary products for the kitchen, which the business became so synonymous with. There is an article in the publication *What to do with our girls; or, Employments for women* in 1884 claiming Alfred as the brainchild behind these concepts:

Ice Cave from *A. B. Marshall's Cookery Book*.

Mr Marshall, being a man of education, has also designed and patented many articles for his wife's requirements, which he supplies at cost price; and he has also devoted his scientific knowledge to the production of concentrated essences and vegetable colours which are perfectly pure and harmless, as certified by an eminent chemist.[27]

The cynic in me immediately assumed that this was just typical Victorian male misogyny, making sweeping assumptions about invention and gender. But this is a book with the specific intention of raising awareness of the need to educate, train, inform, and recruit women, to elevate their status in society. So why would the writer make such assumptions?

An additional mention in the *Lancet* of 1885 also credits Alfred with the invention of the patent cave.[28] A quick check of the patent records does indeed confirm that it is Alfred's name that appears on the 1885 USA granted patent for the ice cave. With the description reading:

A. W. MARSHALL. APPARATUS For FREEZING SOUFFLES AND MOLDING ICE PUDDINGS, am. No. 322,117. Patented July 14, 1885.

UNITED STATES PATENT OFFICE.

ALFRED W. MARSHALL, OF MORTIMER STREET, OVEN DISH SQUARE, COUNTY OF MIDDLESEX, ENGLAND.

ICE-CAVE OR APPARATUS FOR FREEZING SOUFFLES AND MOLDING ICE-PUDDINGS, &c.

SPECIFICATION forming part; of Letters Patent No. 322,117, dated July 14, 1885.

Application filed April 17, 1885. (No model.) Patented in England September 30, 1884, No. 13.007.

To all whom it may concern,.-

Be it known that I, ALFRED WILLIAM MARSHELL-shall, subject of the Queen of Great Britain, residing at Mortimer street, Cavendish Square, in the county of Middlesex,

England, have invented certain new and useful Improvements in Ice-Caves or Apparatus for Freezing Souffles and Moulding Ice-Puddings and the like; also applicable as an ice-safe, and for keeping food or drink at a low or high temperature, of, which the following is a specification.

Up to the present time the moulding of ice puddings and the like has been effected by using moulds, which are made to entirely surround the mixture required to be made into a shape, and to lute with grease or some equivalent every crack and joint of the mould, and then to place the mould into a pail or tub and surround the mould with a freezing mixture, such as a mixture of ice and salt. By my invention I do entirely away with the necessity for specially-designed moulds, and avoid the use of grease or other luting material, and prevent all possibility of brine entering the mould. It also enables the operator to examine the process from time to time & also enables the ice when moulded to be kept ready and be turned out for use at any moment, and also to keep or preserve any part of the ice not used.[29]

Other utensils that Alfred patented include a vegetable washer, vegetable cutters, a julienne cutter, a vegetable ladle, and a vegetable pattern stamp (for giving cut veg a pretty design).[30]

My next assumption was that women might have been prohibited from applying for patents in the 1800s, which would explain why they were in Alfred's name, but it seems this wasn't the case. Alfred did the inventing and Agnes received the credit, although the actual concepts may well be attributed to her. Did the couple work together to carefully construct an image of Agnes as a genius of the culinary world, or did she overshadow Alfred and take advantage of his talents and financial backing? Or was it the other way around? Had Alfred always seen Agnes as a cash cow? We know he had a history of shady dealings and a forceful personality.

Just one year after Agnes died, in 1906 Alfred married Gertrude Walsh. Gertrude was the daughter of the late Captain Ambrose Walsh, RNR of Essex Lodge, Catford.[31] As a young woman in 1891, she worked as a clerk at a school in Camberwell where her mother was the governess and her siblings worked and studied at the same address.[32] Gertrude's social rank must have suddenly taken a dive, as ten years later she was registered as a

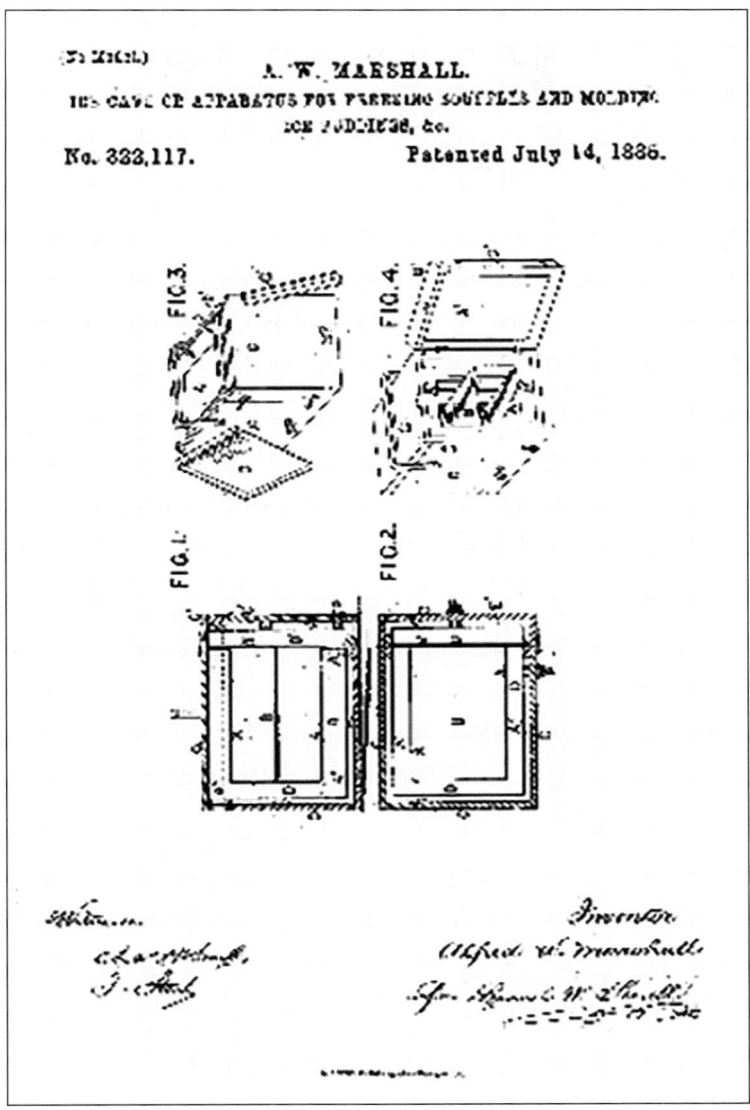

Patent for the Marshall Ice Cave.

dressmaker. Marrying Alfred not only improved her place in society, but it also enabled Gertrude to retrain as both a masseuse and a midwife.

By 1911, having become a father again, Alfred distanced himself from the old family residence of The Towers, to live primarily in Marylebone, London.

THE ENCYCLOPÆDIA OF PRACTICAL COOKERY.

Vegetables—*continued.*

gence, will be understood from the following instructions.

In the first place the cook should see that the Vegetables are quite fresh, for, in spite of anything that may be said to the contrary, all Vegetables, whether roots, leaves, or any other kind, begin to lose bulk and flavour as soon as they are removed from the ground. Those that suffer the least in this respect are roots and tubers, such as carrots and potatoes; and those which suffer most are leaves, stalks, and shoots, such as asparagus, sea-kale, cabbages, and the like.

FIG. 962. VEGETABLE-SLICER (A. B. Marshall).

To clean Vegetables, they should be first soaked for a time in salted water—cabbages and cauliflowers being turned upside-down. In this way the flavour of the Vegetables improves, and all insect life is removed. Next, grit and dirt must be thoroughly washed out, and for this purpose a wire sieve or basket (see Fig. 970) should be used, which may be dipped again and again into a tub of water, the Vegetables in it being shaken thoroughly and rinsed. Root Vegetables offer the artistic cook a very extensive scope for the exercise of skill and ingenuity, as

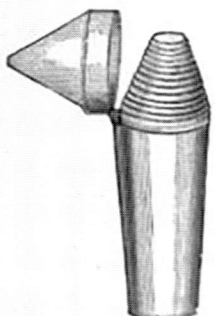

FIG. 963. VEGETABLE-CUTTERS (A. B. Marshall).

may be seen in the numerous shapes and designs into which these Vegetables can be cut. Flowers are often cleverly imitated, and rounds, olives, and lorenge-shapes of every variety are to be seen in artistically prepared soups and garnishes. These require special tools for their production, of which the following may be considered useful examples.

Vegetables—*continued.*

For peeling, some excellent machines have been invented. One of the best (see Fig. 971) acts upon a system of springs. The Vegetable is stuck upon a fork communicating with a handle, the knife being pressed

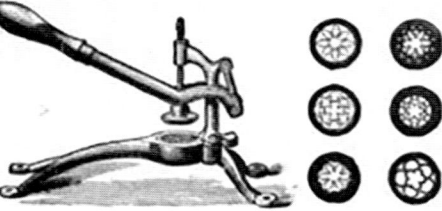

FIG. 962. FANCY PATTERN STAMP (A. B. Marshall).

gently into a convenient position for trimming off the peel as the handle is rotated. Knives fitted with adjustable guards are sometimes used for paring roots, but, as they require a considerable amount of practise to use them successfully, they are not kitchen favourites.

FIG. 963. VEGETABLES FOR JULIENNE.

Vegetables are cut into fancy shapes and designs by the use of various instruments called scoops (see Fig. 972), which produce rounds, ovals, and fluted shapes (see Fig. 973). Spirals or curls of Vegetables are much used for garnishing, and these are produced by means of various instruments (shown in Fig. 974), which fit into one handle.

A variety of this mode of cutting Vegetables is shown in CRULLS (see Fig. 975). Vegetables can be "turned," as it is called, by a dexterous action of the fingers, and the use of a small sharp knife. The mode of proceeding is shown by Fig. 976. This method of preparing Vegetables is of infinite use to the artistic cook for all kinds of dishes in which uniformity of shape and size is a desideratum.

FIG. 964. JULIENNE-CUTTER (A. B. Marshall).

From slices of Vegetables any number of patterns can be cut out (see Fig. 977) by means of cutters or stamps,

FIG. 965. VEGETABLE-LADLE (A. B. Marshall).

which may either be fitted with handles (see Fig. 978), or by simple tubes (see Fig. 979). Either of these styles answers equally well, it being, however, of the first importance that the slices shall be of a uniform thickness.

For details respecting Culinary Processes, Utensils, Sauces, &c., referred to, see under their special heads.

Vegetable utensils from *A. B. Marshall's Cookery Book.*

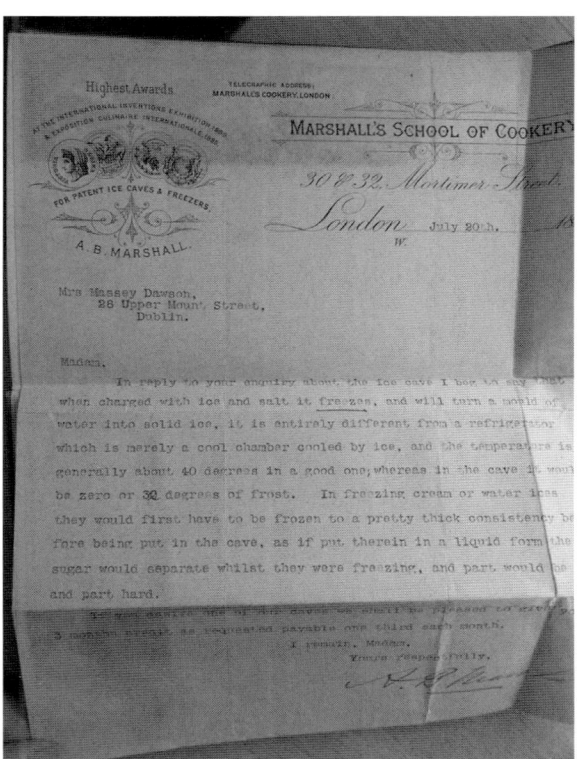

Letter from Agnes to Mrs Masey Dawson re. Ice Cave. (Courtesy of Tony Haynes)

I have read that Alfred and Gertrude Walsh, who was allegedly employed by the Marshalls in some sort of clerical role, were conducting an affair. I can, however, find no evidence of this, although considering Gertrude was living and working as a dressmaker in Marylebone, a mere five-minute walk from Mortimer Street and the cookery school, in 1901, it's not unfeasible that she might have gained employment in some capacity at one of the area's biggest employers before 1905.

In his spare time, and one wonders how he even had any, Alfred Marshall tirelessly fundraised on behalf of the Pinner fire brigade for most of his life, including opening up his house for glamorous garden parties, for which he would charge an entrance fee for the charity itself.[33] He also bought the first working fire engine for Pinner village and became chairman and principal shareholder of Pinner Gas works, expanding this enterprise into Ruislip, Harfield, and Northwood. Alfred was even a councillor for a brief time and was praised for his business acumen and commitment to the local Pinner community across his obituaries.[34]

Gertrude and Alfred's daughter Rosalie Osborne Oliver Marshall was baptised in 1907. She married Nicholas Charles Shelley and they lived their lives in Cornwall with their four children: Charles, Reg, Alice, and David.

In his will, Alfred left nothing to his surviving daughters. He divided his fortune of just under £42,000 (roughly £2.5–3 million) between his son William, his wife Gertrude, two friends, and his own solicitor.[35]

Although this was not unusual in accordance with the way that inheritance rules worked in the nineteenth century, by the time Alfred died, such traditions had become slightly outmoded.

Alfred died in southern France in 1916 at the Riviera Palace Hotel, Cimiez, Nice, while recuperating from an illness. Being wartime, there was a delay with bringing his body back to England and his family had to wait four years to receive his remains, which were re-interred in Pinner Cemetery.

I can't quite work Alfred out. On the one hand, he seems committed, talented, and loyal, on the other, slightly shady, dogmatic, and belligerent. I would like to think that he and Agnes were happy. They certainly made formidable business partners, but was this to the detriment of their marriage and children?

The court case of 1904 in which Alfred relentlessly fought for retribution amid his son's disgraced apprenticeship demonstrates an unwavering arrogance, a compulsion to win. Rather than take the word of an experienced manager and engineer, as well as others who testified, Alfred senior refused to acknowledge the negative aspects of his son's behaviour. These characteristics were even transparent to those in the courtroom, laughing as they did while the unsavoury qualities of both father and son came into question.

The dogged approach Alfred took when handling the thefts from his staff was also slightly manic. People who succeed in business and in life like Alfred often have unbending wills, drive, and a severity of character. I imagine he was forceful and liked to get his own way; whether he was loving and kind with it is impossible to measure.

Marshall's School of Cookery

> Marshall's School of Cookery, is fast becoming one of the most popular institutions in London.[36]

An observation of a lesson recorded by the *Pall Mall Gazette* of 5 May 1888 at Marshall's reveals why it was just so special:

> If cookery can really be made a fine art, Mrs Marshall has certainly succeeded in doing so. Yesterday that lady gave the last of her entire dinner lessons at her School of cookery in Mortimer-street, and during the hours from 10 A.M. till 5 P.M. the class-room where the practical lesson was given was a truly unique and remarkable sight. In the centre of the long room Mrs. Marshall, in her neat, tasteful toilette, worked away with lightning speed at the various preparations which, together, formed a most elaborate dinner menu. All round her the room was crowded with pupils, who followed every movement of their teacher with intense interest, and to whom the ingredients in various stages of perfection were passed for inspection. What makes Mrs. Marshall's performances most interesting is the fact that in all the fanciful dishes for which the average Britisher has, as a rule, only the contemptuous name of 'foreign messes', are prepared in the sight of all men – or rather, all women – so that there is no suspicion as to the natural history of the creature used in a ragout or pie. The most interesting part of the demonstrative lesson is when shortly before four o'clock the whole dinner is 'dished up' ready for table.

Cookery schools before the mid-1800s were limited to private tuition, with some cooks and cookery book writers establishing small makeshift learning hubs in public locations. One of the best examples of this is Edward Kidder, known for his 1721 book *Receipts of Pastry and Cookery*. Kidder taught at a variety of locations around London including Queen Street, East London and Furnival's Inn, Holborn, with a pastry school based in Little Lincoln's Inn Fields. He also offered a service teaching ladies cookery in their own homes.[37]

There were a few examples of small-scale schools, most notably in Luton, which received quite a lot of media attention in the 1850s and a couple of smaller establishments in London, one of which was located at 71 Mortimer Street.

It was the London International Exhibition of 1873 that blazoned the launch of a formal system of learning, based on the success of the lectures and recipe demonstrations delivered during the event itself. The National Training School of Cookery was formed by a group of commissioners and opened its doors in Exhibition Road, South Kensington that same year. The main objectives for establishing a national system of cookery were based on the principles of nourishing and sustaining the labour market, to ensure the wheels of progress continued to turn. There was also a need to coach women for domestic service positions to meet growing demand, and to offer a higher level of culinary art to those working or hoping to work in the kitchens of the elite.

This emphasis on the relevance of cookery in society spurred a whole generation of chefs, educators, schools, cookery writers, and manufacturers of culinary wares. It was big business. Agnes and Alfred were most definitely in the right place at the right time.

Once a stationer and bookshop, then a private residence until 1882, 30 Mortimer Street, Cavendish Square, London was purchased by Agnes and

The National Training School, London. (Taken from *The Lady's Realm* Magazine, 1902)

Alfred and renamed Marshall's School of Cookery in 1883. They initially advertised it as an established business, one that had been running since 1857. I have been unable to find any evidence of this, although there was a very successful cookery school at both number 63 and then 71 Mortimer Street, headed up by French chef and culinary teacher Felix Lavenue. His L'Ecole de Cuisine crops up a few times during the nineteenth century, without significance. Sure enough, an advertisement in the *Morning Post*, 1883, introduces Marshall's School of Cookery, as 'late Lavenue'.[38] I can only assume that Agnes and Alfred purchased the business, but not the premises. Did Agnes know Lavenue socially, had they trained together, or had he even trained her at some stage?

Three years later, this bold entrepreneurial couple extended the business to include the adjoining property, number 32, as the number of those enrolling on courses increased from just forty to two thousand. Despite this, the school had not been an overnight success. On the opening day, no one visited the premises. The following day was the same and so were subsequent days until the Marshalls launched an aggressive advertising campaign, after which one or two pupils enrolled, followed by more as word got around. When Agnes and Alfred embarked on their initiative, there was a scarcity of cooks in England, with just one open position likely to receive in excess of 500 letters from jobseekers.[39] So the Marshalls' assumption that the most dedicated pupils could complete their training as a cook after just three months suited both prospective employees and employers. They also trained existing cooks in new methods and advanced techniques. The cost of training in full could set a student back as much as £21, equivalent to nearly £2,000 in the 1880s. When challenged about the fees, Alfred Marshall became very defensive during an interview in 1886, justifying the high costs as contributing to employment levels and education. He also reacted strongly to the suggestion that the prepared dishes created during the lessons were sold on to hotels or confectioners. Alfred was quick to explain that most wastage was offered to students to take away with them, for the sum of half-a-crown.[40] This was capitalism at its best, certainly not training for the poor, labouring classes.

The school's overall objectives also garnered criticism from more formal sources including the Royal Commission on Elementary Education, which published a report in 1887 damning Marshall's School of Cookery for not having the facilities to train school teachers adequately, despite advertising

Lesson at Marshall's School of Cookery, 1887. (From *A. B. Marshall's Cookery Book*)

to the contrary. The report outlined the lack of specialist teaching provision for children, with too much emphasis placed on high-class cookery and not enough practical instruction nationally. It's true to say that the wealthier classes in Victorian society did not want to encourage education for the masses. There was a fear that too much power would end up in the hands of working-class Britain. A little knowledge goes a long way. Although the government issued grants to help support the largely church-led elementary school system, they did very little else to acknowledge or recognise the importance of education for anyone other than the higher echelons of society. A Royal Commission on the State of Popular Education in England, also known as the Newcastle Report, as it was chaired by the Duke of Newcastle conducted in the late 1850s revealed that only 12 per cent or so of children were receiving any type of formal teaching. The findings of this case study can be found in the Accounts and Papers of the House of Commons for 1862. It would, however, be years before school was made compulsory, in an age when society's main objective was to keep the labour market thriving, with the employment of children being central to this.

By the time the Marshalls had established their cookery school, new Education Acts were in place, with local education authorities taking responsibility for the learning needs of its children aged 5–12. It seems unfortunate that Agnes and Alfred did not take a wider approach to tuition, choosing an exclusive, more lucrative path and failing to offer more mainstream cookery tuition. It's clear the country desperately needed cookery teachers in schools to train young people to cook healthily and economically. Some students signing up with Marshall's would have aspired to a career as a teacher in a new elementary school, but it is clear that the level of training Agnes and Alfred were offering was not suitable for this purpose. Perhaps they just had no need to change the way they taught, or any desire to learn how to adapt, as long as the money kept coming. As the Victorian author Veva Karsland wrote in her report 'Women and their Work' in 1891, the National School of Cookery was running a 'plain cookery teachers' course' for around £10 in 1891, half the cost of what the Marshalls were charging, with the National School of Cookery also insisting that each candidate pass an examination in basic reading, writing, and arithmetic before they could qualify, thereby expanding upon their knowledge and increasing their chances of finding employment. In contrast, pupils studying at the National School learnt how to make Irish stew, beef-steak pie, pickles, treacle pudding, toad-in-the-hole, gingerbread, gruel, beef-teas, and so on. A far cry from Marshall's haute cuisine.

An article about the London school published in *Myra's Journal of Dress and Fashion* on 1 May 1892, ironically written by Isabella Beeton's replacement as editor of *The English Woman's Domestic Magazine* and Samuel Beeton's good friend, Matilda Browne, remarked:

> Among nations, England has never ranked high in the culinary world. It has been cynically said that England possesses 100 religions and only one sauce, and there is a good deal of truth wrapped up in the sneer. As a rule, English people feed, but they do not dine. Their food is generally neither palatable nor digestive unless they borrow the recipes of other nations. The food is either allowed to cook itself in a haphazard fashion, or, if some effort is made to make it palatable and digestive, it is generally at the expense of waste and extravagance. And though the materials for improvement lay ready to the hand or might be culled from the garden hard by, the knowledge of application is usually wanting. How to dress food hygienically and palatably, was and is still, not only amongst the poor but amongst the lower middle classes who have to look to its preparation for themselves, an almost unknown art. All honour is, therefore, due to the late Sir Henry Cole, who first originated the idea of a national school of cookery…

Students in a lesson at the National School of Cookery, renamed the National Training College of Domestic Science, 1944.

Marshall's School of Cookery had five departments:

- The classes – run by Agnes herself daily from 10.30 am–4.00 pm, except Saturdays.
- An agency – recruitment of permanent cooks.
- Hired staff – retain a cook to travel to an event in any part of the country.
- Equipment hire – from an extensive range of catering equipment.
- Stores – selling food, kitchen equipment, utensils, wines, and spirits.

Marshalls wasn't just a school; it was a vast culinary enterprise. During an interview for *The Lady's Realm* magazine of 1902, Agnes implied that the trained cooks who were hired out for private events weren't 'suited to gentlewomen', saying: 'a day cook going into the country for a dinner, leaves her home at 7.30am. and does not return till after midnight. She is "on the go" and standing throughout the long hard day.'

The article concludes that this type of brutal employment was 'better done by women of the domestic servant class'.

Was Agnes so judgemental of women that she felt the need to classify them in this way? Or was it more of a statement about women generally? There were simply those more accustomed to hard graft than others.

The neighbours of Marshall's School of Cookery in 1890 included an architect and surveyor, an art studio and china dealers, while a refuge for young women occupied the building directly next door, reflecting both the capitalist and philanthropic elements of the era.

The strapline boldly attached to the school boasted it was the 'largest and most successful of its kind in the world for high class cookery'.[41] Most publications of the time did not disagree. *The Lady's Pictorial* wrote:

> It is this long and unique training which Mrs. A. B. Marshall has undergone which renders one of her Half-Guinea Lessons BETTER VALUE to a student than any other course of instruction obtainable FOR THE SAME EXPENDITURE OF TIME AND MONEY, and it is not surprising that her School stands a head and shoulders above any similar Training School in the World.[42]

Agnes posing at Marshall's. (Taken from *The Lady's Realm* Magazine, 1902)

The types of dishes Marshall's taught were advertised widely throughout the nineteenth century, offering some insight into what students could have expected to learn:

> Hors d'oeuvres – Various.
> Potage – Consommé a la Ferdinand.
> Poisson – Sole a la Tyrol.
> Entrees – Tournedos a la Mildred, Petites Bombes de veau a la Gelee.
> Releve – Poulet roti – saice Champignons, Pommes de terre a la Piemontaise.
> Sorbet – Sorbet a la St. James.
> Roti – Pintade Piquee – Sauce d'Oranges Glaces, Truffles en Ragout.
> Entremets – Ponding a la Reine, Pompadours a la Milan.[43]
> *Truth*, Volume 33: January–June (London, 1893), 372

Agnes delivering a lesson at Marshall's. (Taken from *The Lady's Realm* Magazine, 1902)

In 1895, the programme of lessons for the week included:

> Monday – New and pretty cold sweets
> Tuesday – Choice fancy savouries
> Wednesday – Best hot entrees
> Thursday – Newest cold entrees
> Friday – pastry dishes.[44]

And three years later:

> Monday July 4 – Breakfast and luncheon dishes
> Tuesday July 5 – Best Hot Entrees
> Wednesday July 8 – Classes Closed
> Thursday July 9 – Choice Fancy Savouries
> Friday July 10 – Dressed Fish and Fish Sauces.[45]

A menu from one of Agnes's lessons on how to cook a dinner was published in 1900 including:

> Hors d'oeuvre: Homard aux olives farcies
> Potage; Consomme a la Carlton

>
> Entrees: Crème a l'Empire; timbale de cailles a l'Empress
> Releves; Quartier g'agneau, sces.menthe, and aux gioseilles rouges;
> Poularde a la St.Vincent.
> Pommes soufflees a la Francaise. Petits pois au beurre.
> Sorbet: Coupe a la princesse.
> Rots: Canetons au cresson; Crème de volaiile a la financiere.
> Salade russe.
> Entremets: Souffle de violettes: mousse au chocolat glacee.
> Biscuits au luxette a la crème. Café noir.[46]

Many of the lessons focused on the French fashion of the time, just like the majority of recipes included in Agnes's books. It's clear that Marshall's market was certainly targeting the middle and higher end of society.

Agnes debuted another special class in 1903 titled 'A Cold Collation', with recipes particularly suitable for weddings, afternoon receptions, and garden parties.[47] The details of what was prepared during these lessons was written up in detail in the Victorian ladies' magazine, *The Queen*. The author of the article, who attended the class, commented on the large number of participants in attendance, praising Agnes's skills and listing some of the highlights including the prawn Mousses a la Moscovite, described as 'dainty little pink moulds served on stands of brown bread and butter masked with mayonnaise aspic, along with chicken and ham creams a l'Alexandra, consisting of ballette moulds lined with chicken puree and set in aspic, served on fine shredded salad, garnished with iced ham cream.'[48]

Traditionally Agnes hosted annual balls alongside supper lessons to launch each new season at the cookery school. This would coincide with a special display of dishes put together by past and present pupils as a sort of exhibition, with other culinary companies such as J. S. Fry exhibiting stalls and holding competitions for the best use of chocolate or the best loaf of bread. Agnes frequently gifted cash to her winners. One year, this event was hosted directly over the road from Marshall's Cookery School at the Cavendish Rooms, although other venues including the Queen's Hall and Langham-Place were also used for this purpose. The individual tables and rooms at these events were arranged beautifully and one can only imagine how glamorous they must have been.[49] We can get a sense of this extravagance from the observations of a journalist attending an exhibition in 1894, which was also staged at the Cavendish Rooms and included a glowing account of Agnes and her successes:

> ... pale pink roses, arranged by themselves, and a regiment of lower vases containing delicate orchids and foliage of all kinds. The centre of the table was occupied by one of the new table fountains, of which an illustration is given, half buried in a bank of orchids and ferns, amongst which darted a covey of shimmering humming birds, so cleverly arranged as to require inspection before one realised that they were not alive, while above it all tinkled the music of a fountain rising to a height of 18 to 20 inches, and diffusing a delicious coolness by its very sound. When the table was fully spread with the dishes and the decorations, it was impossible to avoid being struck by the beauty of the whole, and complimentary opinions were freely expressed on all hands as the eager crowd of spectators entered when the doors of the hall were thrown open at 6 p.m. But a new feature had been added to the show, differentiating it from the equally successful hall supper lesson of hut year, in the shape of a competition between present and former pupils of Mrs A. B. Marshall's school, each competitor showing a three-fold set, consisting of an entree, a sweet, and a savoury, and in some cases – notably in that of the gold and silver medallists – producing dishes that the talented teacher herself need not have disdained to acknowledge as her own production. Indeed, the whole of the entries were of an extremely high standard of excellence, and the difficulties of judging, especially between the two first exhibitors, were really very great. Altogether, it may be said that this competition was one of the most satisfactory parts of the show. Mrs A. B. Marshall's name is not to be made by this time; her skill and talent is generally acknowledged; but this exhibition of her pupils' work shows her in a new light, as the foundress of a really superior school of culinary art, and one which should rank her name among the best-known cordon bleus – an honour alike to her sex and her nation. Such an exhibition as that held last Tuesday and Wednesday week should go far towards teaching even our very

conservative housekeepers and cooks that cooking is an art of the most delicate kind, and one which makes as great claims on its professors as the verist enthusiast for painting, music, or sculpture could claim; and if this specimen of cookery in tempts even a proportion of our ladies to take an interest in such a pretty art, we have even more cause, for gratitude to Mrs A. B. Marshall than we have as yet acknowledged, or even possibly realised.[50]

The supper lesson itself was delivered by Agnes and each year it would feature numerous complicated dishes that she would demonstrate individually in front of a very large audience, who were once described as 'eager and excited'.[51] Her supper lessons of 7 and 8 May 1894 included a demonstration of how to prepare and cook the following exotic-sounding dishes:

1. Potable d la Marguerite. 2. Saumon la Riviera – Sauce S'erte Glade. 3. Pith; de Gibier a la Francaise. 4. Jambon la Cielee. 5. Filets de Sole a l'Adelaide. 6. Petite' Teases de liomard it la Duc de York. 7. Eufs de Pluviers la Louisville. 8. Chaudfroiti de Ili. de Veau A la Coburg. 9. Msuviettes In Clifden. 10. Chiudfroid de Cailles la Manta. 11. Creme de Legumes Is Valentine. 12. Kari de Vo!Mlle la Marie. 13. Artichauts la Portland. 14. Petite Criem de Lasalle Marlborough. 15. Sandwiches d In Madras. 16. Ssudwiches et Biscuits au Luxette. 17. Salado la Metropole. 18. Petits Babas la Marie. 19. Ihmphines au Chocolat la Crime. 20. Petite. Corbinlles de Nougat It la firer. 21. Petite. Crimes a la Vienne. 22. Baba aux Fruits A la Duchesse. 23. Petites Gelees A la Berlin. 24. Macedoine de Fruits en Gelee. 25. ielee & la Russe. 26. Pompadours. 27. Gel, nu Ithum 'Silver Rays.' 28. Café A la Francaise. T.l. Glace de Clique de Fraises et Eau de Citron.[52]

Observations of Agnes by the media noted:

How the talented lady preserved even an appearance of composure was a marvel to the spectator, but that she did so was evident, and a very keen consciousness of the requirements of the several dishes, too, as she turned now and again to give directions for the attentions to he paid to various things which had left her skilful fingers for their final preparation on the fire, in the ice cave, or the oven, or paused to help a willing but not always competent volunteer assistant in some unexpected problem, returning quietly to the point under her own special care with unruffled clear-headedness, as if she had never been stopped. This power of giving her attention to points foreign to the work at the moment under her hands, and rerunning the latter, after a five minutes' divergence, at the exact point at which she left it, without a second's confusion, is one of the chief factors in Mrs A. B. Marshall's success as a cookery teacher. An ordinary woman would grow confused between sweets and savouries, solids and kickshaws, and find it difficult, if not actually impossible, to resume the thread of her previous demonstration; but not so Mrs Marshall, who appears able to follow the fate of half a dozen dishes at least in her mind, without confusing their details, or entangling the methods of their preparation, keeping a perfect pace of their various needs, and realising the exact moment when each will next require attention from her, as if that particular item was the sole and singular point on her mind. To judge by this supper, it is clear that the day of grosses pieces is nearly if not actually over; indeed Mrs A. B. Marshall did not concern herself for such things…[53]

In 1898, the cookery school announced it would close one day a week, on Wednesdays, throughout the summer months. By the following year, this extended to full summer closure from the end of July until the beginning of September. Whether this was the Marshalls' need to take a regular vacation from their hectic schedules, or a reflection of Victorian society as a whole extending its leisure time, is unclear, but it must certainly have been difficult for Agnes and Alfred, running all their separate enterprises with a large family at home. There were ongoing advertisements for cooks (women) and chefs (men) required at Marshall's in its prime, suggesting the business either couldn't retain its staff, or simply operated beyond its capacity.

Agnes explaining the uses of utensils at Marshall's. (Taken from *The Lady's Realm* Magazine, 1902)

When Agnes died, another Agnes, Agnes Myhill, took over the teaching at Marshall's. Myhill was a former pupil of Marshall's, taught from the age of 16. She initially worked at the cookery school in an assistant capacity and was probably mentored by Agnes personally.

During one of her classes at Marshall's in 1925, Myhill, along with her assistants, made the following dishes to a packed room of students. It seems they were still peddling the high level of French cooking well into the twentieth century. Although the heavy dishes of the Victorian and

Edwardian eras were still popular, particularly among the aristocracy in England at this time, things were changing. Not least of all with influences from America and a move towards fresher, lighter, and more importantly, dishes that took less time to prepare and eat. These menus would have started to look somewhat outdated.

Hors oeuvre.
Coupes a la Cumberland Potage.
Consomme a la Karachi
Poissons.
Fillets de Merlan a la Monigue.
Parfait de saumon en Gelee.

Entries'
Cotelettes de Veau a l'Auguste.
Caneton Farci a la Montreuil.
Releve'
Langue de Boeuf Chaude. Sauce Dubois.

Entremets.
Mousseline d'Ananas a' la Crème.
Petites Gondoles a' la Bon Don.
Biscuit Glaci a' la Rose.[54]

The school of cookery continued to advertise for staff in *The Times*, up until 1941, seeking instructors in ration cooking during the Second World War.[55] After this time, there are no further references to the school in the media; it simply became another casualty of war.

Work away from the cookery school

Agnes's recipes were being recreated in the homes of the fashionable London glitterati, as described in a society column of the *To-Day* magazine, 1895, with the writer describing a dish she ate while dining with the 'Henry's' – 'The salmon trout was such a pretty dish, being dressed in fillets each in the form of a tiny pink salmon, and laid on a circle of aspic jelly, the centre of which was filled with lettuce hearts cut small, and dressed with a delicious cream sauce. It was one of Mrs. A.B. Marshall's.'[56]

Agnes was commended and revered throughout Victorian society. We must not dismiss the significant impact she made, with a reputation once associated with culinary excellence throughout the country. She was all things traditional and grounded in her knowledge of cookery, but also innovative and progressive.

Agnes's shortcut convenience products were heavily endorsed across all her works – gelatine, ground almonds, baking powder, food colourings, sauces, cooked rice flour (a thickening agent), vinegars, concentrated consommé, curry powder, coralline pepper, icing sugar, fruit syrups, even cane sugar. The list goes on. One of her most popular retail items was Luxette, a savoury spread sold in a shallow earthenware terrine.[57]

Advertisement for Luxette.

Whether she developed these products herself, or Alfred did, is unclear. He did class himself a gelatine merchant in later life and was noted in several publications for his inventions. I could offer numerous examples of advertisements for all these products, but they simply represent a time in which many new labour-saving, utility foods were entering the market. They would have been in high demand and sold competitively alongside countless other similar brands at the time.

Along with the ice freezer and ice cave, the Marshalls' enterprise manufactured cabinet refrigerators, which were large wooden glorified cool boxes, a range of moulds for just about any type of ice, blancmange, jelly, or liquid that could be set in a pewter or tin shape.

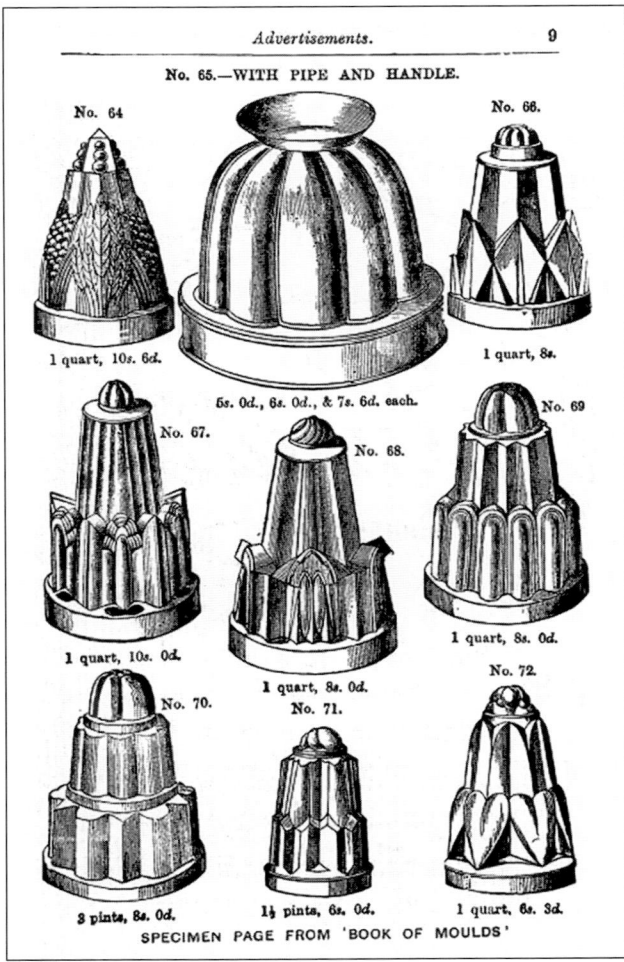

Moulds from *A. B. Marshall's Cookery Book*.

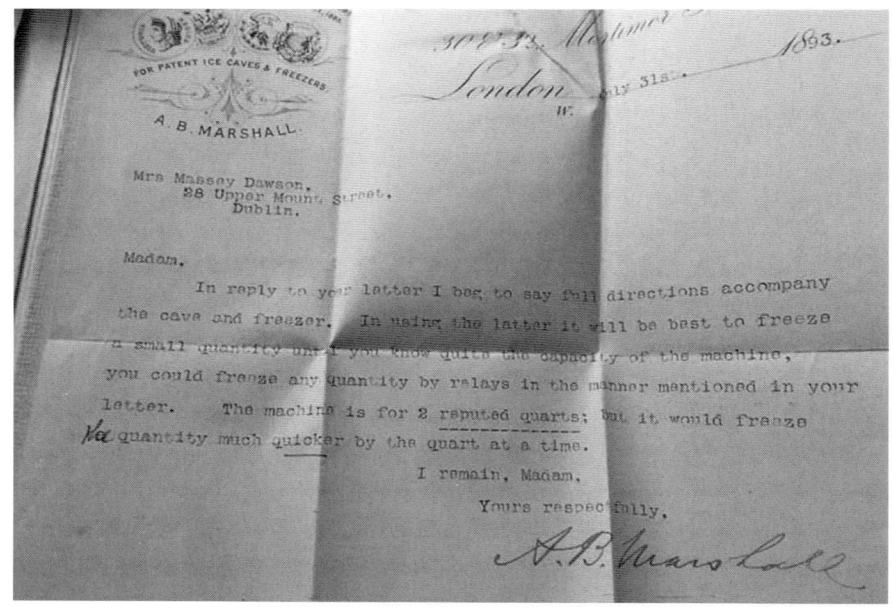

Letter from Agnes to Mrs Masey Dawson re. Ice Cave. (Courtesy of Tony Haynes)

In 1886, Agnes chose another direction for promoting her work, which became a mouthpiece for personal views, launching her weekly magazine *The Table*. This little paper included anything from scraps of titillating gossip to subjects she enjoyed like horse riding and tennis, along with her recipes, most of which were reproduced in her books. Again, it wasn't unusual to write a periodical like this in the nineteenth century. Mrs Beeton herself was adept at it and the market was flooded with printed literature, a bit like apps and podcasts today. But it was the sheer body of work that Agnes churned out that demands admiration. As well as *The Table* magazine, Agnes Marshall wrote a couple of academic papers, contributed to a few publications, and wrote four books: *Ices Plain and Fancy: The Book of Ices* (1885, reissued 2018), *Mrs A. B. Marshall's Book of Cookery* (1888), *Mrs A. B. Marshall's Larger Cookery Book of Extra Recipes* (1891), and her *Fancy Ices* (1894). All this on top of creating an internationally recognised cookery school, brand of cooking ingredients, endless lecture tours and ground-breaking inventions, before the age of 50. Not to mention the four children she raised, although raised is probably an overstatement, considering she and Alfred would never have been around to spend time with them.

THE TABLE.

THE TABLE, which was established in the early half of the year 1886, and is now in the fourth year of its existence, was published with the view to supplying what was then felt to be a great and growing want — a family paper which should assume the position of an authoritative guide on the much neglected subject of gastronomy, treated from an entirely practical standpoint.

The immediate and gratifying support which was accorded to the venture led, at the completion of the first year of publication, to the material enlargement of the paper, and the addition of various important features, which, while still giving prominence to its original *raison*, assimilated it in all important respects to the society journal, which has become so important a feature in our modern life. The process of development has been consistently carried out, and at the present time THE TABLE may claim to occupy a unique position as an organ which, while supplying a large fund of information of indisputable value to the family, supplements it with a record of society doings and social and artistic gossip, which aims at being authoritative without being scandalous, and can be exact without experiencing the necessity of being improper. The present important features of THE TABLE may be summarised as follows:

GASTRONOMY.

Under this head may be primarily included the weekly contributions of Mrs. A. B. Marshall, of Marshall's School of Cookery—a collection of new, original, and high-class recipes of *recherché* dishes, specially written for THE TABLE, the copyright of which is vested in its proprietors. These average about 300 recipes in each volume, which represent alone the contents of a high-class cookery-book more than equal in value to the price of the entire volume. To this feature has been added a page of Answers to Correspondents on practical details connected with the cuisine, which are furnished by Mrs. Hamilton, a *diplomée* of Mrs. Marshall's School of Cookery and a recognised authority on the subject.

A practical illustration of modern gastronomical ideas is furnished by the publication of a collection of *menus* of recent public and private dinners of especial excellence, both French and English.

From time to time other collections of recipes by competent authors are published, and, for the guidance of housewives, a weekly Retail Market Table is given, with notes compiled from information furnished by the leading West-end retailers.

Articles on Food, both in its popular and scientific aspects, are furnished by writers of authority, and a notice is given of all Household Novelties which have been submitted to the management and severely tested.

Wines, spirits, and other beverages, being subjects cognate to food, articles on these are constantly given, and the authority with which these are written has been recognised by the inclusion of many of them, with due acknowledgment in recently published text-books.

TABLE AND HOUSEHOLD DECORATION.

This being a subject which of late years has acquired great importance, the proprietors of THE TABLE have enlisted the services of Mrs. Allen Simpson, a lady who combines great native taste with an intimate acquaintance with the fashion prevalent in the highest society, and a persevering pursuit of the latest novelties produced by the manufacturing houses.

Mrs. Allen-Simpson also conducts a Correspondence Column for the benefit of her readers, and the success of her writings is attested by the support given to the paper by a large number of Transatlantic trade buyers of glass, china, and *objets d'art*, who find in her articles hints of greater value to them than are afforded by the regular trade journals.

DRESS AND FASHION.

As this subject cannot be otherwise than important in a family paper, Mrs. Armstrong, a lady of established reputation as a writer of taste and discernment, supplies a weekly article, which comprises notices of the latest fashions as displayed at society functions, and the latest novelties at the leading London and Paris houses, to which is added a column of Answers to Correspondents.

SOCIETY.

The social information published in THE TABLE is supplied by accomplished writers, who enjoy the exceptional advantage of mixing in the circles whose doings they chronicle.

MUSICAL, DRAMATIC, & LITERARY.

The musical criticism in THE TABLE was made an important feature in the paper by the late Dr. Francis Hueffer the first critic of his day, and has, since his lamented death, been conducted on lines not unworthy of his initiation. The literary and dramatic criticism has been submitted to competent hands, and is written from an entirely independent standpoint. Notes on subjects of current interest are included in the Table Talk.

CITY ARTICLES.

The proprietors, having special sources of information, including correspondents in America and the Transvaal, have arranged for the publication of special articles of interest to investors, and criticisms of current ventures conceived without bias and written without fear or favour.

FICTION.

Under this section a weekly Table Tale by an author of note is published.

THE TABLE enjoys a circulation of exceptional strength. Its subscription list is probably larger than that of any London weekly paper, and includes families of wealth and position in every part of the kingdom. It is taken at all the leading clubs and hotels in town and country, and offers exceptional advantages to advertisers who appeal either to the family or to first-class business houses.

Edition of *The Table*, 1889.

The next chapter provides a little more insight into *The Table* and an in-depth analysis of her books, one of which *Mrs A. B. Marshall's Cookery Book*, it's safe to say prompted some fairly enviable reviews:

Manchester Guardian – 'This may justly claim to be, and is in fact the most interesting and important cookery book that has been issued for a great many years in England.'

Birmingham Gazette – 'There is no doubt that this addition to the list of cookery books will achieve popularity and attain the rank of a standard work.'

Leeds Mercury – 'Here is a volume of the kind that may fairly lay claim to originality, and that has the rarer merit even of absolute trustworthiness.'

Even Queen Victoria herself commented on *Mrs A. B. Marshall's Cookery Book* in 1893: (*Morning Post*, 30 January), noting:

> It is certainly, both for the variety of its contents and the perfection with which it is got up, the finest specimen of English cookery literature that has hitherto appeared. The illustrations are a study in themselves … A book fit to take its place on the shelf with the standard culinary works of Gouffe, Francatelli, Urban Dubois and Ude.[58]

You couldn't get a much higher endorsement than that in Victorian England.

In 1888, Agnes and Alfred toured the United States. While based in Chicago, one newspaper described her, rather insultingly, instead of a successful woman in her own right, as the 'Miss Parloa of England' (a US cookery book author, owner of cookery schools and culinary lecturer). The article said little about the work Agnes was carrying out while over there, choosing rather to focus on her physical appearance, as 'a brunette of fine form and bearing, under middle age, with the ruddy complexion that characterises English women … and speaks with a marked English accent'.[59] In fact, sadly, this is all that any newspaper in the US appears to have said about her visit that year.

Just as it is today, it was tough cracking the US market in the 1800s. Once it was cracked, however, America could offer a wealth of new commercial opportunities. Unfortunately, it's not clear exactly what elements of the business Agnes and Alfred were promoting on their tour, although according to an article in *The Lady's Realm* magazine of 1902, she taught cookery in New York City at some stage in her career. Perhaps the couple were trying to establish future potential. Many UK businesses sought insight and inspiration, knowledge exchange, and of course enterprising expansion across the Atlantic in the nineteenth century. This was not uncommon, but it seems the Marshalls may have failed in this particular area if they were anticipating overseas growth.

Two years earlier, in 1886, Agnes and Alfred also embarked on a European tour in order to acquire a knowledge of new and inspiring dishes served in Vienna, Ratisbon, Cologne, Dresden, Berlin, and Prague among other locations.[60]

Only a few months before this trip, the Marshalls were once again embroiled in a court case, this time facing the accused William Waudley for sending letters to Agnes reproaching her for overlooking his wife's application of employment. The alleged letters Waudley sent were of 'a very objectionable character', speaking libellously about Marshall's School of Cookery. Whether the case was brought to trial as propaganda for the school, or once again the Marshalls felt the need to publicly chastise someone for trying to get the better of them, is up for debate. We do, however, know that William Waudley was a former inmate at East Riding Asylum and the process of dragging such a vulnerable man through the courts is somewhat implausible.[61]

Ever on the treadmill of success, the couple toured the UK provinces the following year as part of Marshall's 'A Pretty Luncheon' initiative. One such lecture delivered in Birmingham was written up in a local newspaper. Agnes, together with two assistants and Alfred interjecting from time to time, prepared a lunch menu including lobster mayonnaise, pigeons, grilled chicken, parmesan souffle, French omelette, maraschino jelly, nougats, and strawberry and vanilla creams. These dishes were then served to audience members to sample after the two-and-a-half-hour demonstration. It was observed that Agnes's attire remained spotless throughout, despite all the whisking, beating, and boiling. Every participant was provided with printed versions of all the recipes to take away with them.[62]

Six years on and Agnes embarked on yet another regional tour, lecturing on the merits of cooking with gas. She used a Richmond and

Co range throughout her demonstrations.[63] The Richmond Company was established by Edmund Walter Tyrell Richmond in 1889 so the tour was undoubtedly one of mutual endorsement. In 1892/93, she coincided these gas demonstrations with a series of practical lectures titled 'A Tempting Repast'.[64] Once again, her husband accompanied her on this tour. His role was to interpret and demonstrate Marshall's range of utensils and kitchen equipment.[65] I have found records of Agnes delivering this particular lecture series across Dundee, Hull, York, Leeds, and Newcastle. Reserved seats cost 2 or 3s, unreserved were 1s. This would be equivalent of between five and twelve pounds. According to the *Truth* periodical, Agnes made the following dishes during this lecture tour: grouse, a couple of savouries, jelly, an ice, and nougats.[66]

She certainly seemed relentless in the art of self-promotion, but Alfred was always there by her side, on every tour. Was he there to ensure the smooth running of events, or simply offer support? Was it gender oppression, emotional comfort, or purely practical chaperoning? Perhaps it was all of these things.

After her death, Agnes was described as 'a pretty woman, of a Spanish type, with large, dark, kindly and expressive eyes. Her figure was slight and graceful'.[67] She was said to be quiet and gentle.

This same journalist had attended one of Agnes's classes, remarking:

> She possessed that not very common gift, a discriminating and sensitive palate. Men often say that women have no palate, but if so, there are a few exceptions to the rule, and Mrs Marshall was a notable one. Her Friday class, to whom she gave a practical demonstration of cooking a whole dinner of many courses was a tour de force ... She stood in the centre of a long table, which was surrounded by cooks of almost every age and size, and her manner was as quiet, her gentle smile as composed, as though she were merely preparing tea for a few friends.[68]

There is plenty of written evidence to suggest that Agnes was a patient, kind, and devoted advocate of her craft. It's her unflappable qualities which really seem to have roused admiration. I envisage Agnes as someone almost bewitching her pupils and audiences, with the phrase 'a steady hand on the tiller' springing to mind.

The Dundee Advertiser called Agnes 'strikingly handsome', 'graceful', even going so far as to christen her 'the high priestess of cookery'.[69]

Agnes was not without humour either, as a witty little retort she wrote in response to the *Caterer* periodical of 1885 indicates. Agnes was asked by a correspondent what she thought about the coffee served in France. She claimed to be amused by placards displaying statements referring to coffee frequently displayed by London grocers including:

> A luxury unknown in England.
> French Coffee, as used in Paris, in its highest perfection.
> 10d. per lb.

Adding:

> On the adjoining window I see a printed and highly eulogistic extract from a London weekly. The editor of the said paper has doubtless thoroughly sampled the material he speaks so highly of, and if your correspondent cannot take his word for its excellence, I fear there is no alternative but for you to send him a sample, as I have not tasted it. Of course you could taste it yourself instead of him if you felt so disposed; and perhaps he would prefer you to.

Agnes went on to say:

> I have had some very good coffee in Paris and some very bad. The best I have had was in London, and also the worst; but I think a stranger would be more likely to be pleased with the coffee in our first-class restaurants than with that in the best-known Parisian cafes, taking a given number in each city. Notwithstanding this, the following little incident did happen in London:
>
> 'Waiter', called an old gent, 'here what's this?'
> 'Coffee, sir; 6d., sir.' 'Coffee! not this.' 'The cup sir? We don't sell the cup sir.' 'Don't you be impertinent, sir. What's the stuff in the cup?' 'Coffee, sir; 6d, sir.' 'I tell you it isn't.' 'I'll

fetch the Manager sir.' Manager: 'Coffee not good, sir! It's generally so much liked. What are the grounds of complaint?' 'No grounds of coffee, sir. It's extract, extract and hot water, and an attempt to extract 6d. out of my pocket. They got me to taste it once at a show, and I shan't forget it. No, No.' Yours faithfully. A. B. Marshall. Marshall's School of cookery. Mortimer Street. September 3, 1885.[70]

Today Agnes would undoubtedly have been in receipt of some sort of order of merit and in 1886 she was actually awarded a 100-guinea diamond locket by her pupils at the cookery school, with the ceremony presided over by a member of parliament.[71]

Whether Agnes worked in the kitchens of the wealthy or started her life in a stimulating educational environment that would inspire her drive for knowledge and success is still unclear. In reality, she has a meagre legacy, and despite her name being familiar among those with an interest in cooking and historical cookery, she remains an unknown entity.

It is hoped this book will do a little to rectify that.

Brown and white painted portrait of Agnes.

Chapter 2

The Recipes and Innovations of Agnes Bertha Marshall

If you are looking for recipes published in Marshall's editions of *The Table* magazine, you won't find many in this chapter, as it focuses on Agnes's best-known works. This is largely because having spent a little time researching the recipes published in the *Table*, it seems many of them coincide with the existing recipes to be found in Agnes's books, like this one from a January edition of *The Table* in 1889, which is lifted directly from *Mrs A. B. Marshall's Cookery Book*.

> **Puree of Spinach**
> Take two pounds of fresh spinach, pick the stalks off and well wash it, then put it in a saucepan and cover with cold water; add a good pinch of salt and a tiny piece of soda; bring to the boil quickly, keeping it pressed down under the water with a spoon; when it boils strain into a colander or a sieve; rinse with cold water, then press it and rub through a coarse wire sieve, or chop it very fine; when passed put it in a clean stewpan with two ounces of butter, a tiny dust of pepper, salt and sugar, and one tablespoon of flour that has been passed through a sieve; mix up well together, then add two good tablespoonfuls of cream or good gravy; stir till it boils, then use.[1]

Spinach was known for being wholesome in the nineteenth century, but strangely in the 1890s it was also thought not to be terribly nourishing, in that it wasn't considered beneficial to health, growth, or wellness in any way. Typically it was boiled, creamed, pureed, or pressed into a mould to provide a decorative outer layer for jellies or poached eggs. Gravy was its favoured companion and the French were fond of adding nutmeg and white wine to many spinach dishes, something Agnes has chosen to omit here, favouring a more English type of preparation.

Compilations of *The Table* weekly editions are available as reference books, by prior arrangement, at both the British Library and the National Trust.

Neither does this book include any recipes from the exceedingly rare *Fruit and Vegetable Bottling at Home: Fruit Preserving Without Sugar*, published long after Agnes's death by Marshall's School of Cookery in 1917 with a reprint in the 1920s. Or the even more elusive *Apple Cookery: Various Ways of Cooking Apples and Methods of Utilising this Fruit in Several Different Dainty Dishes*, published in 1923, again under Agnes's name.

There is one other archived title to my knowledge associated with Agnes and that is 'Illustrations of high-class entrées given in the lecture hall, Royal Aquarium, December 17th, 1885 / by Mrs. A.B. Marshall', which appears to exist as a single sheet of notes/drawings that currently resides in the care of the University of Cambridge Libraries.

I do, however, want to mention a literary reference to Marshall by the outlandish culinary legend Fanny Craddock in *The Sherlock Holmes Cookbook*. This is a truly eccentric work written in the guise of Mrs Hudson, the fictional housekeeper of Sherlock Holmes and Dr Watson. Fanny narrates a series of recipes as Mrs Hudson, many of which are inspired by Hudson's imagined training with Agnes Bertha Marshall. Fanny actually illustrates a very realistic picture of her idealised image of both Agnes and the training rooms at Marshall's School of Cookery. Allegedly Fanny Craddock had proposed a book based around Agnes and her work, which would have been titled *The Great Marshall Mystery*, suggesting the circumstances around her death were suspicious. The book failed to reach the publication stage as it lacked any credible research material. Fanny's response was that Agnes's husband Alfred had conspired to prevent its publication, despite the fact that he'd been dead some sixty years or so. In reality, Agnes had been ill for a considerable time with carcinoma synoptic, or lung cancer, and had not recovered from the fall due to further complications with this same illness.

The Sherlock Holmes Cookbook contains some of Agnes's recipes, Fanny's recipes, and those of other chefs including Escoffier.[2]

Taken from this rather rare to find book, the following extract is Fanny's imagined participation in one of Agnes's classes, through the eyes of the fictional character of Mrs Hudson (yes, it is that surreal).

Apple Fritters as they should be made
I never make these fritters without recalling my wonderful experience of sitting among the pupil-audience for one of the great Mrs Agnes Bertha Marshall's cooking classes. We all crowded eagerly together in benches which were so raised about a cleared area below, that even the ones on the topmost rung were able to see this lovely and gifted lady as she cooked and instructed throughout a memorable day. She wore a charming morning dress with, as I recall a very elegant, braided ruff about the hem. Yet so orderly and so precise was she that never a speck fell upon the floor to soil that pretty hem. Nor did she wear what any of us working cooks would consider to be an apron; but only a little fancy, frilled thing which she tied about her slender waist.

   Now I have never made my batters with egg, milk and a little water. Mrs Marshall soon showed me the error of my ways. First she prepared the apples, sound Bramleys of course, by pairing away the skin extremely finely and then using one of the modern apple core removers to thrust down centrally and withdraw again with all the core therein. These she then sliced a half inch thick so that they resembled apple rings, just fresh ones instead of the dried ones with which we were all familiar. She then summoned a member of the audience to assist her. 'Pray prepare the steeping agent', she requested of this person whom I longed to be but was too shy for such exposure to all those pairs of eyes. This consisted of the strained juice of 1 lemon to offset discolouration, followed by a large tablespoon of inexpensive cooking brandy and 1 tablespoon of sugar. 'Now we will make a batter which will really puff them up beautifully every time'. So saying she measured off 4 heaped tablespoons of superfine self-raising flour into a basin. Then she made a well in the centre, pit in 1 tablespoon of olive oil and thinned the mixture down to a very thick batter consistency with cold water. Having so done she covered this springy paste with a plate and let it lie until the thirty minutes had elapsed, when she gave her assistant 2 egg whites to whip stiffly, proving that they were so, for all of our entertainment, by turning the bowlful upside down over her elegantly dressed hair. Finally she folded and cut the egg whites into the stiff batter, thus making it a trifle looser. Then the apple rings were drained over a sieve so that the juices ran down into a small bowl. Each apple ring was then drawn through the batter until completely coated. For this she employed the blunt end of a wooden skewer and thus lifted the ring into her deep pan of almost smoking hot, pure olive oil. 'You must so regulate the oil heat', she explained, 'as to ensure the batter and apple are cooked right through.' Adding, 'they *are* done when a rich golden brown'. She dredged them on pieces of crumpled tissue paper, set them in a fine line, overlapping down a silver dish covered with a dainty paper doyley and at the last, passed a sieve of icing sugar over the tops, tapping the side with one finger as she did so to ensure even distribution. To my surprise she then poured the soaking fluids into a very small copper saucepan, added 2 dessertspoonful's [sic] of apricot puree, stirred both over a strong heat – she performed with a modern gas stove – and when hot poured in another tablespoon of brandy and turned it into a pretty chased silver jug. 'And thus send to table', she ended.[3]

Although Fanny has picked up on the Victorian trend to use more olive oil in cooking, as Agnes certainly did, it is very doubtful, as with most chefs of this era, that she would have deep fried anything other than fish in olive oil, certainly not apple fritters. Clarified butter or fat was nearly always used for deep frying. Neither did Agnes's standard batter for fritters include milk; she did, however, fold whisked egg whites into her yolks, flour, and water.

Fritters have a heritage that extends to at least Roman times – the Latin for fried is *frictura* – but they became most popular during the medieval period. It's one of those dishes that shifts between countries and cultures – think Indian pakora, Japanese tempura, or German Apfelkuchle. Apple fritters were even once traditionally eaten on Shrove Tuesday. While pancakes prevail, that particular custom bowed out sadly. We're all familiar with the nursery rhyme that pays homage to this:

Oranges and lemons
Say the bells of St Clement's.
Bull's eyes and targets,
Say the bells of St Margaret's.
Brickbats and tiles,
Say the bells of St Giles.
Half-pence and farthings,
Say the bells of St Martin's.
Pancakes and fritters,
Say the bells of St Peter's.

Pick up most basic cookery books of the Victorian era and you will find a recipe for apple fritters.

Agnes also contributed to a book published by the North Midland School of Cookery, titled *Home Cookery*, in 1893. The recipes she provided are variations of those found elsewhere in her books, but she obviously came to an agreement with the publishers to include as many favourable mentions of her leaf gelatine as possible, which is recommended throughout, possibly in exchange for the inclusion of her recipes.

This was not an isolated practice, as Agnes's books are lavished with advertisements for all the products that contributed to the Marshall empire.

In the preface to her publication from 1888, *Mrs A. B. Marshall's Cookery Book*, Agnes emphasises that with all her recipes, 'I have written each accordingly, and have not copied from other authors … they are the result of practical training and lessons, through several years, from leading English and continental authorities, as well as a home experience earlier than I can recall.'

The word continental might suggest a variety of countries other than just Europe, but sadly, despite the odd reference in articles, we will probably never know exactly where or how Agnes trained, but we do know she must have been very young when she started.

Agnes eulogises that 'stock is the foundation of all cookery'.[4] It is of course the base for most sauces and the Victorian culinary era was certainly passionate about sauces, particularly the rich, heavy French and European approaches to sauce making. Allemande, or German sauce, was very fashionable, along with bechamel, espagnole, hollandaise, and tomato sauces.

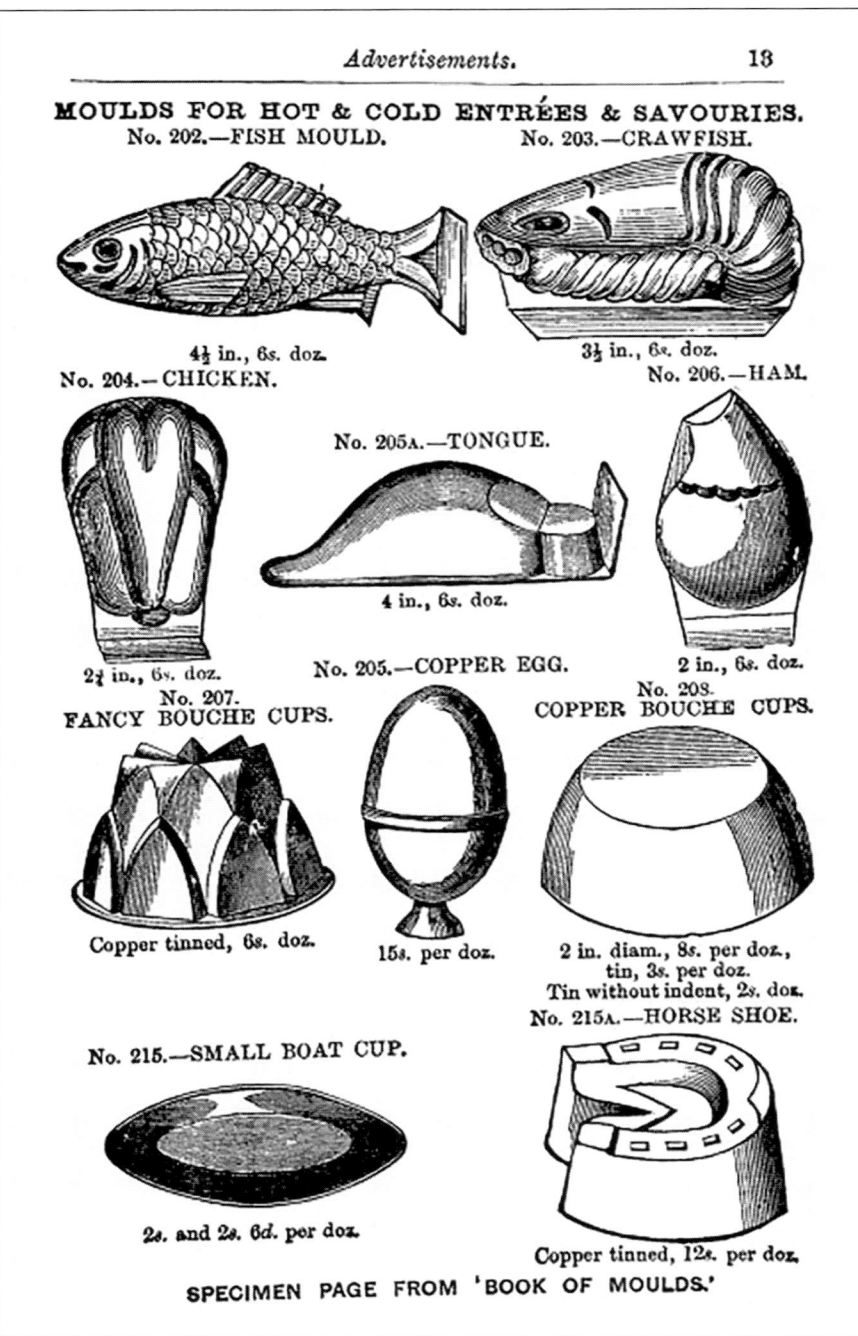

Cold entrées and savouries from *A. B. Marshall's Cookery Book*.

Here is Marshall's version of Allemande sauce, which differs significantly to that of Auguste Escoffier's. Agnes suggests mushroom liquor, as opposed to whole mushrooms; she then instructs on melting butter in the pan before adding the ingredients separately, while Escoffier adds everything at once, advising that butter must only be added at the end of cooking to avoid the sauce turning or separating. Auguste Escoffier was becoming one of the leading chefs of his generation when Agnes was at the height of her fame. His famous *Le Guide Culinaire* was published just before she died. Despite referencing big nineteenth-century names in the culinary world like Jules Gouffe, Urbain Dubois, Baron Brisse, and Alexandre Dumas, there is interestingly no mention of Escoffier in any of her books, neither does Agnes ever refer to Isabella Beeton.

Allemande sauce
Put two and a half ounces of butter into a stewpan with two and a half ounces of fine flour, and fry together without discolouring, then mix it with one and a half pints of good-flavoured white stock, either from veal, rabbit, or chicken, stir till it boils, then add a quarter of a pint of washed fresh white mushrooms that have been cut in thin slices, boil for about fifteen minutes, then stir in four raw yolks of eggs that have been mixed with a gill of thick cream, a dust of coralline pepper, and the juice of half a lemon; stir the sauce over the fire again until it thickens, then have it rubbed through a clean tammy cloth and use.[5]

The version of Allemande sauce published in Mrs Beeton's original 1861 *Book of Household Management* is called Sauce Tournee, which she notes was the original name for a velouté. When thickened with egg yolks, this then becomes the distinctive German sauce, so we can learn the evolution of this recipe from Beeton, which is one of the many advantages to her work.

While Agnes, like many of England's establishments at that time, was preoccupied with French cuisine, she was also partial to throwing in a simplified dish among her chapters, to appease some of her less skilled readers, or those disinclined towards 'foreign foods'. I also favour her chapter devoted to English into French translations, which not only reduces the level of pomposity, but acknowledges Agnes's understanding of her wider, less knowledgeable readers. There was a deep division with concerns relating to overseas influences, including food, during the nineteenth century among the British people, across all classes. Victorian dinners often lasted hours and consisted of numerous courses, including soups, entrées, and then heavy meat and accompanying vegetable dishes. Then there were palate-cleansing ices, followed by more meat and desserts, and closing entremets, which consisted of anything from sweets to small savoury dishes.

One recipe for boiled salmon appears simple and yet there was seemingly considerable variation with the methods of cooking this dish in the Victorian era, with some debate as to whether the fish should be added to cold or boiling water at the start of cooking. Agnes suggests pre-boiled water with vinegar and salt. Some recipes of this era also instruct that the fish itself should be covered or encased in something prior to cooking, to protect its fragility. Beeton advises to just drop the fish in as it comes into cold water.

My 'go to' authority on all methods of cooking is *Larousse Gastronomique*. Originally published by its namesake, *Editions Larousse*, in the late 1930s, this encyclopaedia of gastronomy was a collation of mostly French recipes contributed by some of the most famous chefs of the time including Georges Auguste Escoffier. It has become a global classic reference book for cooking techniques and in recent years has been greatly updated to include a broader selection of recipes and additional culinary material. My own 1961 edition stipulates that salmon, when being boiled, should not be immersed into water containing any herbs or condiments, in line with Mrs Beeton's version but contrary to Agnes's own recipe. It does not state whether the fish should be protected from the direct effects of the water or not, although I suspect this is because it's probably not required.[6]

Other discrepancies are apparent with Marshall's recipes, like her Chicken Fricassee. Jules Gouffe, who was one-time protegee of Antonin Careme as well as being the brother of Queen Victoria's pastry cook, Alphonse Gouffe, stresses the importance of using young fowl for this dish, in order to retain tenderness and freshness, as well as emphasising the importance of quick blanching. This is corroborated by Mrs Beeton in her *Book of Household Management*. Agnes mentions neither, in fact she instructs the reader to pre-boil the chicken for thirty minutes. Gouffee states that anything more than blanching the chicken joints at that stage 'will only spoil it, and destroy the flavour'.[7]

It's curious that Agnes doesn't seem to apply a fundamental cooking technique here, which may be indicative of her training.

> **Pigeon and Beefsteak Pie (Pate de Pigeon et Boeuf)**
> Pick, singe, and bone the pigeons, and cut each bird into four pieces; take four birds to one pound of fillet of beef or rump steak, cut the latter in little square pieces, and season all with chopped bayleaf, thyme and parsley, chopped eschalot, a little salt and pepper; put into a buttered saute pan and fry together for eight or ten minutes, then mix in a tablespoonful of flour, put all into the pie dish, fill the dish with good gravy, and garnish the top with halves of hard-boiled eggs and button mushrooms that are masked with a little chopped parsley, cover the pie with puff paste, glaze the paste over with whole beaten-up egg, mark the top with a knife, and bake in a moderate oven for about two hours. Serve hot or cold for a remove or for a luncheon dish. Any kind of game or poultry can be used in the same manner.[8]

Isabella Beeton includes an 'Epsom Grand-Stand Recipe' for pigeon and steak pie in her 1861 *Book of Household Management*, so presumably this was one of the rare recipes which might have belonged to the Beeton family household. While Marshall leaves us clueless about quantities, Beeton as ever provides those useful details including quantities, average cost, the number of people it's likely to serve, and the recommended season to cook the recipe. Eliza Acton, another rather forgotten culinary practitioner and writer of the Victorian era, who has gained greater notoriety in recent years, proposes nutmeg and mace as the main seasonings, which is unusual. I'm not sure how nice that would be and, like Agnes, she advocates the inclusion of pre-hard-boiled eggs, in contrast to Beeton's whole raw eggs.[9]

I find Agnes's to be the superior recipe for this dish, purely because her seasoning is more compatible and she includes mushrooms as a standard ingredient, as opposed to Acton's 'alternative' suggestion and Beeton's absence of mushrooms all together. Mushrooms as far as I'm concerned provide a meaty flavoursome accompaniment to all game and steak pies.

As far as I know, hard-boiled eggs were (and still are) often added to pastry or baked goods to make the final dish less tough and chewy. Historically they have also played a decorative role in some raised pies. As for the addition of raw egg yolks, I'm not sure how this would work and imagine the result to be quite a custardy texture, which doesn't sound that appealing.

Pigeon Pie (Epsom Grand-Stand Recipe)
Ingredients – 1¼ lb. of rump-steak, 2 or 3 pigeons, 3 slices of ham, pepper and salt to taste, 2oz. of butter, 4 eggs, puff crust.

Mode. – Cut the steak into pieces about 3 inches square, and with it line the bottom of a pie-dish, seasoning it well with pepper and salt. Clean the pigeon, rub them with pepper and salt inside and out, and put into the body of each rather more than ½ oz. butter; lay them on the steak, and a piece of ham on each pigeon. Add the yolks of 4 eggs, and half fill the dish with stock; place a border of puff paste round the edge of the dish, put on the cover, and ornament it in any way that may be preferred. Clean three of the feet, and place them in a hole made in the crust at the top: this shows what kind of pie it is. Glaze the crust, that is to say, brush it over with the yolk of an egg, – and bake it in a well-heated oven for about 1 ¼ hour. When liked, a seasoning of pounded mace may be added.

Time. – 1¼ hour, or rather less.   *Average cost*, 5s.3d.

Sufficient for 5 or 6 persons.   *Seasonable* at any time.[10]

Game pies have been popular since medieval times and young pigeons in particular were kept as fodder for the plate in Britain, Africa, and the Middle East. In Victorian England, pigeons were broiled, stewed, curried, jugged, roasted, and made into puddings. It was a versatile and popular choice for the dinner table. It was also important to source young birds, cooked as soon as they were culled if they were bred and tamed for the table, or hung for a few days if they were wood pigeons. The darker the plumage, the higher the flavour and the better the quality if eaten between June and September.

When Agnes boasted about never copying recipes, only recreating those that were once imparted to her by various tutors throughout her many unknown years of training, she was seemingly not being untruthful. An article published in *The Cheltenham Examiner* dedicated to Agnes after her death reveals the location of 10,000 collated recipes stored in the basement of Marshall's School of Cookery, recipes which were Agnes's 'sole conception'.

Some of these recipes, written on an early typewriter, were sold at auction some years ago, purchased by collector Anthony Haynes, a few of the images of which his wife contributed to this book.[11] They have since been sold on again. There are certainly recipes published in her books which I have seen nowhere else, not reproduced in any texts I know of published in Britain. This includes dishes like Haddock a la Marta, essentially baked haddock served with a bechamel sauce made from the cooking juices of the fish, to which shrimps and anchovies are added. While there are many versions of haddock served with shrimp sauces, I can find none quite like this. And there are countless examples like Salad a la Nuremburg, a delicious-sounding chicken, anchovy, and olive salad, dressed with herbs, chilli, gherkins, and hard-boiled eggs, which is also misspelt if we are to assume she meant the German city, Nuremberg. Then there's Cauliflowers a la Kahlenberg, coating the cauliflower in bechamel sauce, before sprinkling with blanched carrots, turnips, and parsley. And the majestic Pudding in Surprise a la

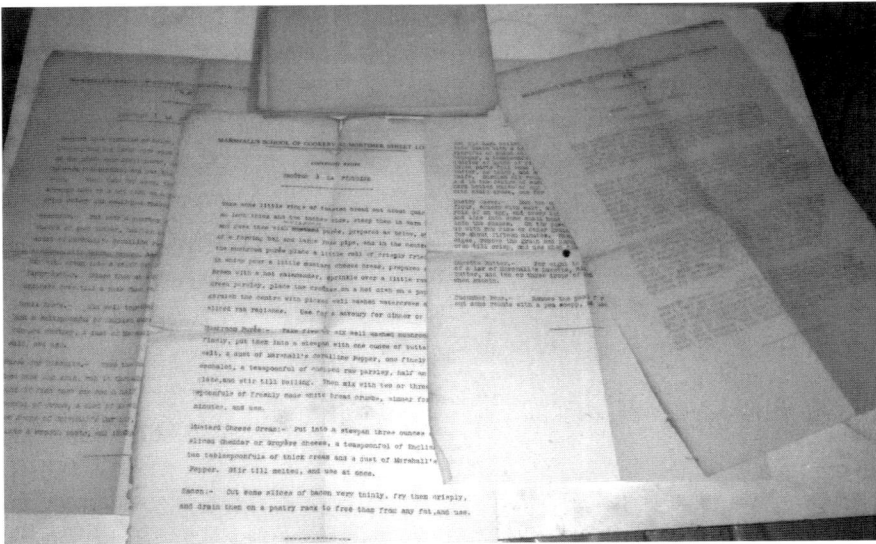

Selection of Agnes's typed recipes. (Courtesy of Tony Haynes)

Recreation of Agnes's Macaroni Gratin. (© Emma Kay)

Louise – think a really rich summer pudding containing glacé cherries, which is inserted into an elaborate and ornamental jelly. From an interview with Alfred Marshall in 1886, we glean that Agnes invented a clear mulligatawny soup for Lord Dufferin during a dinner served at the Northbrook India Club, which the gentlemen present decided to christen la Dufferin, in his honour and in recognition of how good the soup was.[12]

Agnes's more familiar recipes, to appease the less advanced cook, include staples like Parsley Sauce, Oxtail Soup, Puff and Short Crust Pastry, Pound Cake, Yorkshire Tea Cakes, Household Bread, Welsh Rarebit, Cheese Straws, and Oat Cake, to name a few, and my particular favourite, Macaroni Cheese, a dish recognised in England since medieval times, popularised in the 1700s and positively mainstream by the Victorian era.

Macaroni au Gratin

Put a quarter of a pound of Naples macaroni into boiling water, season with a little salt, and cook for twenty minutes; when cooked strain off and put into cold water similarly seasoned till required for use, then cut it in lengths of about one and a half inches; butter the dish on which it is to be served, and place on it a thick layer of good Bechamel sauce in which some grated Parmesan has been mixed … arrange the macaroni on that, and put more of the sauce over the top; this is best done by using a forcing bag and large rose pipe for the purpose; sprinkle a few browned breadcrumbs over it and put a few small pieces of butter here and there on the top, stand the dish in a tin containing boiling water, and let it cook in a quick oven for fifteen to twenty minutes; when about to serve brown the top with a salamander, and send to table boiling hot as a second course or luncheon dish. For the above quantity of macaroni take a pint of thick Bechamel sauce and mix into it a quarter of a pound of grated parmesan cheese, and a good dust of coralline pepper. This will make a dish for six to eight persons.[13]

While most of us probably add cheddar or other relatively inexpensive hard block cheese to macaroni these days, in the nineteenth century it was nearly always parmesan. Possibly a pairing of early medieval origins, certainly in Italy anyway, with cheeses similar to parmesan also produced in Anglo-Saxon England, macaroni and parmesan became a dish most familiar to the Georgians who discovered it on their grand tours of Europe and brought it back to England. Macaroni became a more generic term for the wigged, powdered, and extravagantly dressed dandies of the eighteenth century who were inspired by bold continental fashions. Parmesan was an expensive luxury necessity among the wealthy. Pepys is known for hiding his during the Great Fire of London, while even earlier Tudor kings and queens were gifted it to sustain overseas relations.

Agnes flaunts her knowledge of chefs, recipe writers, and culinary literature of the past in a section towards the end of her *Cookery Book* when she writes in detail about the composition of menus while demonstrating a knowledge of dining throughout Europe – Russia and particularly France.

While you could argue that Beeton provides more useful and often essential tips on preparation, timings, and seasonality after each recipe, the lengthy section towards the back of Agnes's *Cookery Book* also details the specifics of meat and vegetables, how to choose your cuts, and so on. To her the recipes themselves clearly took precedence, while meal compositions, seasonal choices, and the selection of produce was of secondary importance and she omits this information altogether in her *Larger Cookery Book*.

Marshall's magazine *The Table* also provided an ongoing dialogue of culinary advice, like this recommendation in an 1893 edition for keeping meat cool in hot weather, albeit a tad elaborate:

> Get some stiff crinoline steels, and make a large circular bag of tarlatan or leno muslin, enclosing the steels (or canes do very well) at intervals up the sides, so as to keep them evenly distended. Get a carpenter to make you a piece of strong wood in the shape of the letter X, with an iron ring fastened to the centre above, and a galvanised meat-hook underneath the end of each arm of the cross. You will hang a joint or piece of meat to each of the four hooks, and tie your crinoline bag, which should have a running string at the top, round the base of the ring, and thus you can hang up your meat safe from flies anywhere. To prevent it getting bad buy some powdered charcoal, and fill a few bags with it, letting them hang closely round the meat, and you will thus be able to keep it sweet nearly a week. If meat gets tainted, always wash it over with a little salt and water, or vinegar, before cooking, basting it with the same whilst roasting.[14]

By 1895, Marshall's *Cookery Book* was in its '30th thousand' edition according to the *Pall Mall Gazette* of 18 May 1895. I assume they meant it had sold 30,000 copies. The article continues with a lengthy, interesting, and very descriptive, if somewhat pretentious critique of the book itself:

> Too much cannot be written and printed and published upon a subject so all-engrossing, so triumphantly inexhaustible. Novels may pall, verse may clot, history and biography may bore beyond endurance. But the cookery book is as fresh today as it seemed yesterday; nor by tomorrow can it have lost its interest, Open Mrs. Marshall's where you will, and names and dishes endeared by memory and gay with promise give you joyful greeting. Now, it may be filets de sole a la Normande; now laitue a l'espagnole; and again, filet de boeuf aux truffles or sardines a la Cambridge. Without reading further, have you not here beautiful food for dreams as you sit by your fire

through the long winter evenings, or as you lie on the soft, crisp grass of your garden in the sunny summer mornings?

But it is not the dream alone that is to be fashioned from Mrs Marshall's volume. Its object is wholly practical; she is the Baedeker of active kitchen, rather than the Murray of winter fires and summer gardens. Some five hundred pages she has filled with recipes, and it is her proud boast that there is not one among them which has not put to the test and found worthy. Is not this a glorious record? Take each page, count the number of recipes upon it; take each recipe and reckon the length of time essential to its preparation, from the moment market is visited until the conquering dish is set upon the table; consider, then, the interval spent in eating; and finally, sum up the whole, and you may know to the minute how many hours and days and weeks and months and years of happiness of surely the most fortunate being of the age. Why bother about female suffrage? Why grow excited over the equality of the sexes? Why seek to be new, emancipated or anything else unpleasant, when, in the compiling of cookery books, woman has ever at hand her supreme chance in a world that need not necessarily be a vale of tears, without one redeeming ray of sunshine? A few breakfasts and dinners and suppers are given in a chapter to themselves, and here Mrs. Marshall's wisdom fails. There is a suggestion of brutality, in her breakfasts especially that might well have been omitted. To sit down at noon, and, with never a prelude, never a gentle warning, whether in guise of blushing radish or flaming tomato, of curving anchovy or estimable eel, have cutlet or beefsteak or chicken thrust before one, is to feel appetite waver at the outset. Where, for instance, is the motive, the scheme, the artistic composition in this menu for a dejeuner for twelve persons: coteleties de mouton pains; lapin a l'Allemande; viands froides; croquettes de poison; pommes de terre a la maitre d'hotel; haricots verts; tarte de cerise? It reads like cold bill of fare in restaurant or hotel. There is no revelation of the master mind, of the creative artist, the symmetrical-breakfast, like the beautiful decoration, is never without its motive, never without its arrangement in accord

> with the eternal laws of art. Did the Botticellis, the Giottos fling paint on the walls they painted with no thought, no care for the rhythms of line, of form, of colour? And as with the mural decoration so with the successful breakfast. The menu should lead up gently from the light to the more substantial, and then as gently down again to the light. Cutlet, or beefsteak, or chicken should represent the highest or most substantial note struck; if it be made to serve for the light prelude, think of the horror and confusion that must inevitably ensue. Not enough is to know how to cook; not enough is to have command of rare variety. Unless the banquet as a whole be perfect as each of its several courses, then will it have been served in vain. As a gulf may be fixed between painter and artist, so also artist and cook may be as the poles apart. To Mrs. Marshall's 'Glossary of terms' all praise must be given. It does not pretend to be as exhaustive as Mr. Senn's 'Culinary Dictionary'. But with its limits it is excellent. There are certain words which continually occur in English recipes as in French, so continually, indeed that compilers take the reader's or the student's knowledge for granted, and vouchsafe no explanation. Mrs Marshall, however, leaves no chance for ignorance; and she who knows not what a bain-marie may be, or what a chaudfroid, to whom quenelles and nouilles are mysteries as strange as Eleusinian rites, need but turn to the Glossary to shake off ignorance for evermore. A Food calendar – who would exchange it for the Shakespeare calendar of convention? – and an Index add to the usefulness of a useful book.

If this was indicative of Agnes's readers, customers, and pupils, then she had a tough crowd. Underneath all that pomposity in this review is a strange mix of someone who demands cookery as a superior art form, but who is also struggling with its terminology.

Although I write about the history of food, I have never identified with the community of people who completely immerse themselves in food as a specialism, the mastery of its presentation and obsession with precision. I'm just as happy in a Pizza Express as I might be in the Savoy Grill. I also feel a bit like an impostor within that world as somebody looking in, enviously observing the endless critiques, meticulousness, and passionate analysis of the look, smell, taste, quality, and quantity of food, recipes, and the dishes themselves. What lights my fire is to know how it got on the plate, what its origins are and whether it's always been paired with one thing, but never another. Who typically eats it and who typically ate it or prepared it long ago and why.

I don't relate to food defined as a symphony. Taste is unique and everybody's tastebuds differ. My husband cannot taste fish unless it's smothered in herbs or sauce and even then, it's the latter he's tasting, not the fish itself. He generically determines the texture of all seafood as rubbery and is unable to find any redeeming qualities in eggs or mushrooms. It's not that he dislikes any of these things, he is just completely unable to find any flavour in them. Tastebuds are individual, so pairing one food that is supposed to complement another is never going to work for everyone. It's like offering dietary tips, everybody's gut and metabolism is different. A diet that works effectively for one person may be useless to another, and so on.

What this review article does highlight, however, which is quite interesting for the Victorian period, is the notion of breakfast and lunch dishes. In the century before, breakfast might involve spiced bread and cakes, hot chocolate, and rolls, bread and butter and preserves, perhaps a little meat and cheese. It wasn't particularly substantial. In the early 1700s, wealthier classes dined between 9.00 and 10.00 am, sometimes even as late as 12.00 pm, with dinner (yes, dinner in the daytime, it wasn't just a Northern thing either) between 2.00 or 3.00 pm. Later in the century, this had shifted to anywhere between 7.00 and 9.00 pm, leaving a considerable gap between breakfast and the evening meal. Typically, the Georgians wouldn't have eaten a formal lunch as breakfast was often served late, but they would have had a light meal for sustenance. Sometimes this was referred to as nuncheon. Lunch became a standard meal in the nineteenth century. As Mrs Beeton mentions in her *Book of Household Management*:

> This is a very necessary meal between an early breakfast and a late dinner, as a healthy person, with good exercise, should have a fresh supply of food once in four hours. It should be a light meal; but its solidity must, of course, be, in some degree, proportionate to the time it is intended to enable you to wait for dinner…

For these 'light' meals, Isabella recommended potted ham, hare or chicken, pig's face, cold fowl in a mayonnaise sauce, broiled partridge or pheasant, baked mushrooms, and slices of cold meat among other dishes. Amidst all the large, complicated place setting lunches for twelve, Agnes, in her 1890 edition of *Mrs A. B. Marshall's Cookery Book*, does also suggest simple dishes such as oxtail, beef and vegetables, salmon in a creamy cheese sauce, or game-based kromeskies, which are a rather splendid blend of French and Polish minced meat or fish croquettes.

> **Kromeskies a la Polonaise**
> Cut up half a small eschalot and put it in a stewpan, add four good tablespoonfuls of brown sauce and half an ounce of glaze, and reduce this to half the quantity, then mix in about four tablespoonfuls of any cooked game or poultry, cut up in thin shreds about an inch long, also about one tablespoonful of lean ham or tongue, one or two truffles, three or four button mushrooms, all cut up in the same manner; when the whole is well mixed, put it aside to cool and get firm. Take some very thin slices of fat bacon, each about two and a half inches square, put about one teaspoonful of the mixture on each slice of fat, and wrap it up in the shape of a cork, taking care to close up well the ends of the bacon; then deep each in batter, and fry in boiling fat till a nice golden colour and quite crisp. Dish on a dish-paper and garnish with fried parsley.

As for the Victorian breakfast, for the wealthy it tended to reflect their enjoyment of visiting guests with large sideboard buffets of toast, buttered muffins, kidneys, bacon, boiled and poached eggs, potted meats, cold ham and tongue, and seasonal fruits in spring and summer, all laid out self-service style. For the working classes, it was street food and a hot drink en route to a day of industrial hard labour.

Agnes, as ever, had some rather more interesting breakfast suggestions in her *Cookery Book* including the intriguingly sounding 'Ham Butter'. Essentially this was well-seasoned cooked cold ham, mashed together with hard-boiled egg and lots of butter before being sieved finely. I guess it worked as a sort of makeshift pate. Alternatively cooked brains, marinated herrings stuffed with hard-boiled eggs, seasoned with tarragon, and brushed with aspic, breadcrumbed and fried spelts, whiting with anchovy butter, boiled mackerel in a fennel sauce, fricasseed chicken legs, curried and devilled chicken, steak, hashed beef, and one of my absolute favourites, Bubble and Squeak.

Originally, Bubble Squeak was simply cold boiled cabbage which was fried up and served under or on the side of a plate of beef (preferably salted beef). This was also either fried separately or eaten cold from the previous day's meal. It had no potatoes, onion, or other greens added to it.

It has been quoted frequently as dating back to 1806, in a recipe published by Maria Rundle, but I found a much earlier reference of 1777 in *The Lady's Assistant for Regulating and Supplying her Table* by Charlotte Mason. This Bubble and Squeak recipe is mentioned as being a good one to use for slightly undercooked boiled beef.

The 'bubble' is the sound of the cabbage being boiled in water and the squeak is the sound that cold, well-drained cabbage makes when it hits a hot pan. In those days, you have to remember, frying pans were very different to the ones we have today. Cooks used cast-iron skillets or griddles (crude pans, often no handles) that sat over an open fire, so they got very hot indeed, hence the squeak of the cabbage.

The early nineteenth-century chef William Kitchiner actually wrote a piece of music to the recipe for Bubble and Squeak, with a song published in his book the *Cook's Oracle* that went: 'When midst the frying pan in accents savage, the beef so surly, quarrels with the cabbage.'

By the 1820s, it was common to add a sauce of pickles and melted butter and the former head chef to Queen Victoria, Charles Francatelli, in his book *The Modern Cook*, added a brown sauce, which incidentally wouldn't have been anything like your standard 'HP' variety, to his fried cabbage and beef Bubble and Squeak recipe. Many of the recipes he included in this same book were prepared for the Queen herself.

Here's Agnes's breakfast (or lunch) recipe:

Bubble and Squeak
Take some thinly cut slices of cold boiled salt beef (fat and lean) and sprinkle over it a very little black pepper; put a piece of butter or clean beef dripping into a saute or frying pan, make it hot, then put the slices of beef into it, and fry them on both sides till a pretty golden colour; then take up and put

the pieces of meat between two plates and keep them hot over boiling water till ready to dish up. Have a nice fresh cabbage plainly boiled and pressed from the water; chop it up finely on a clean board, then put it into the pan in which the beef was fried and fry it for about five minutes; turn it out in the centre of a hot dish on which it is to be served and arrange the fried slices of beef round, and serve very hot.

The *Larger Cookery Book*

Marshall's *Larger Cookery Book* boasts newly invented recipes, which have all been tested and are duplicate-free of her original book. Many of the dishes were illustrated, nearly 300 in all, during Agnes's classes. This adds considerable value to the recipes themselves. In fact, the book itself appears to be a fairly valuable asset all round, with *The Cheltenham Examiner* confirming it was priced at 22s. In the 1890s, this would have been equivalent to about £80.[15] Perhaps this is a good place to mention that books in the nineteenth century, although prolific, were not essential items. Your average family probably only had a couple of shillings a week spare if they were lucky enough to have anything at all. As the century progressed, industrial print production increased and copyright laws became more flexible, many texts could be republished and sold at greatly reduced prices for wider markets, after retailing at a premium cost for about six months or so. This would still amount to several shillings, though, and was not consistent with the sale of all books. Around half the population of England – both male and female – were also illiterate up until the mid to latter part of the 1800s, when literacy levels began to rise more steadily. Whatever the price, however, Mrs Marshall's *Larger Cookery Book*, according to Barbara Ketcham Wheaton, went on to sell some 60,000 copies. Within what time frame is not clear.[16]

Marshall's Cookery School had showrooms dedicated to all the kitchenware they manufactured. It was a place where the public could go and look at the huge range of designs of culinary moulds, knives, and cutlery, etc., make notes, and study Agnes's recipe books. It would have looked a lot like a study library and must have been ideal for those who either couldn't afford her books or were able to observe illustrations as well as the Kitchenalia itself to better understand some of the techniques.

Marshall's Mortimer Street Showrooms.

Never one to miss a marketing opportunity, Agnes referenced her own branded coralline pepper some 321 times in her standard cookery book and again roughly 315 times in her larger book. She described it as 'a natural pepper, of a brilliant red colour, pleasant and delicate flavour, quite distinct from cayenne'. One assumes that it was probably similar to a mild paprika.[17]

The coralline is mainly included in sauce recipes or for giving hors d'oeuvres a bit of punch, like this one for Cashews a la Diable (Devil's Cashews).

Cashews a la Diable
Take some cashew-nuts, allowing about a dozen to each person, and throw them into some clarified oil or butter in a stewpan, and fry them till a nice golden colour; put them into a strainer to drain from the oil, season with a little coralline pepper and salt, dish them up on a dish paper, and serve for hors d'oeuvre, savoury, or dessert.[18]

The significant number of sauce recipes included in this book is testament to a time when the sauce was clearly everything to a meal. One of my favourites is Agnes's *Good Man Sauce.*

Good Man Sauce (Bon Homme Sauce)
Take one tablespoonful of strained lemon juice, two tablespoonfuls of mushroom liquor, four ounces of grated Gruyere or Cheddar cheese, a teaspoonful of French mustard, the same of English mustard, one gill and a half of tomato sauce, half a wineglass of sherry, a teaspoonful of Luxette; stir all together over the fire till boiling and quite smooth, and use for any kind of fish, steak etc.[19]

If you're wondering what Luxette was, I can clarify that it was a sort of fishy sandwich spread and savoury puree, invented and manufactured in dainty little porcelain pots by the Marshall commercial merry-go-round and sold widely in grocery stores, or by post.

Agnes's *Larger Cookery Book* was dedicated to Princess Christian Schleswig-Holstein, formerly princess Helena, the fifth child of Queen Victoria and Prince Albert. Whether this meant that the two women, who were only about ten years apart in age, were closely acquainted is unclear. Princess Christian was an advocate for women's rights and as such I would like to think that the two shared a mutual passion for this cause. We do know that the princess was due to attend one of Agnes's lectures at the Albert Institute, Windsor in December 1887, but had to pull out at the last minute due to a prior engagement.[20] Princess Christian was apparently adept at making jam and had been taught to cook as a child by Queen Victoria's kitchen staff.[21]

Agnes was also captured by the celebrity photographer and photographer to Queen Victoria herself, W. & D. Downey, sometime in the 1880s or 90s. She certainly was moving around in the right circles of society.

I particularly like the section on 'Buns, Breads, Cakes ETC' to be found in the *Larger Cookery Book* which includes numerous medieval recipes from Whigs to wafers, Marchpane (marzipan), and even barley bread, combined with more nineteenth-century contemporary Victoria cakes and Geneva Rolls. It is once again a reflection of Agnes's broad knowledge of historical culinary practices.

From Medieval Europe to contemporary America, Agnes clearly gained some inspiration from her visits to the United States to include such recipes as Philadelphia and Chicago Doughnuts, flannel cakes, and deep-fried Saratoga

Emma Kay making marchpane using Victorian methods.

potatoes. Saratoga potatoes is an established American recipe, although the principle is basically potato chips, or crisps as the British call them, a concept which has a complicated heritage, with ownership attributed to everyone from US president Thomas Jefferson to various cooks working at the Moon's Lake House restaurant in Saratoga Springs (hence the name), to English chef William Kitchener. We will probably never know for sure who the first person was to thinly slice and deep fry potatoes, but they have become more synonymous with United States culinary culture over time and would have been very popular by the 1890s, when Agnes's book was first published.

> **Saratoga Potatoes (Pommes de Terre a la Saratoga)**
> Take some washed and peeled potatoes and cut them in thin slices with a vegetable slicer; dry them in a clean cloth; lay them in a frying-basket (but not overlapping each other) and plunge them into hot frying fat, which must cover them completely; cook till tender, then take up the potatoes and allow the fat to boil up again; then plunge the basketful in if the fat is enough to cover, till the slices are crisp and a pale golden colour; shake from the fat, season with salt, sprinkle with a little chopped parsley, and serve. The above may also be served cold; and they may also be sprinkled over with a little castor sugar and finely-chopped lemon-peel and served as a sweet. They will keep some time, and can be put to warm in the oven when wanted for use.[22]

The *Book of Ices*

Agnes's *Book of Ices* was released in tandem with the launch of her patent freezer, during a period when the consumption of ices of all kinds, from savoury vegetable ices, to sorbets, iced waters and cream ices (ice creams), were the height of fashion. The mixtures were originally poured into a pewter lidded sabotiere or sorbetière, which was rotated slowly by hand in a wooden barrel containing ice and salt. An ice spaddle or houlette was also used to pound down the ingredients being mixed together in the sorbetière every now and then. Both these items were possibly invented as early as the 1600s in Italy.

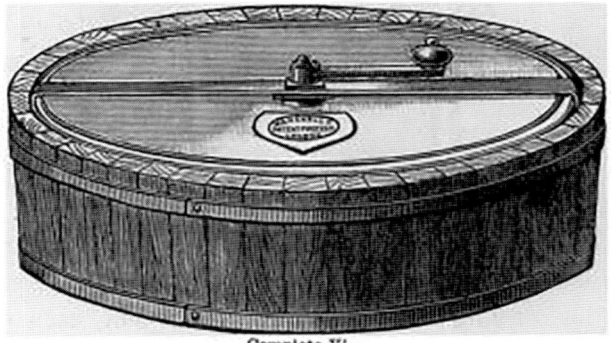

Marshall's Patent Freezer. (From *A. B. Marshall's Cookery Book*)

From eighteenth-century cookery writer Hannah Glasse we get a sense of how ice cream was being made domestically in Britain at this time from her book *The Complete Confectioner*:

The Method of Icing all Sorts of liquid Compositions
When your composition is put in the sabotiere take some natural ice and put it in a mortar when it is reduced to a powder strew over it two or three handfuls of salt then take your pails put some pounded ice in the bottom and place your sabotiere in those pails which you fill up after with ice to bury the sabotiere in. You must take care in the beginning to open your sabotiere in order not to let the sides freeze first and on the contrary detach with a pewter spoon all the flakes which stick to the sides in order to make it congeal equally all over in the pot then work them well for they are much more mellow by being well worked and their delicacy depends entirely upon it. Do not wait till they are thoroughly iced to begin to work them because they would become too hard and it is not possible to dissolve what is congealed in lumps or pieces when you see they are well congealed let them rest taking care for this time there should be some which stick to the sides of the icing pot this will prevent them from melting and make them keep longer in a right degree of icing is. If your composition does not congeal so quickly as you wish through the melting of your pounded ice you may change that ice in the same manner as you put it before for as there is always a hole at the bottom of those pails you may let the water of your melted ice run off by taking out the stopper without disturbing the sabotiere then fill your pails up again as you did before continuing rolling your sabotiere till you see the composition is congealed to the point you wish.

The Method of moulding Ices in all Sorts of Fruits
When your composition is perfectly congealed take a spoon and the moulds you want to make use of fill these well with your ices as expeditious as you can you must have besides ready by you a pail with pounded natural ice and a great deal

of salt there put your moulds in proportion as you fill them and cover them directly with pounded ice and salt continuing so doing to every mould you fill up till you have filled them all when that is done cover them quite and set them a full hour in that ice when you want to take off what is in your moulds take a pan of water and first wash well those moulds one after another to rub off all the salt which sticks round them then open your moulds and put their contents in a disli and send them up. You may give to every one of your ices the very colour of the fruit they represent thus have your colour ready by you and with a very fine pencil point them quickly in which case they must likewise be served directly or at least you must put them in the cave your cave must have been set in a pail and prepared half an hour before you take your fruits from their moulds in that cave you are then to set them after they are coloured till the time comes of serving them your fruit is certainly much finer and takes more the downy look of the natural one.

Victorian objects for making ice cream from the collection of Emma Kay. (© Emma Kay)

What Agnes's patent zinc-lined freezer did was to minimise the laborious efforts required of the bucket and sabotiere. There was a pan on a tub. Pounded ice and salt were added to the tub and the pan inserted on the pivot of the tub. The ingredients were then poured into a little door in the lid of the pan and the handle was cranked to churn the mixture round. There was no need to pack ice and salt around it. After two to three minutes of turning the mix using the handle, you could observe how much it had frozen by peering in through the door , continuing to rotate the handle if necessary until it had sufficiently frozen. Then you could simply shovel it into your mould of choice.

Her ice cave, which was essentially a metal box placed inside a wooden chest, served as a device for freezing the moulds themselves. You'd place the moulds inside the cave which had a compartment which you'd pack with ice and salt, before placing the moulds inside on a shelf for anywhere between one and a half and three hours to set.

Here is Agnes's simple, yet quite decadent recipe for apple ice cream. By sheer fluke, I actually discovered that I had an empty bottle of Marshall's 'sap green' food colouring in my extensive collection of Kitchenalia, which I acquired years ago as part of a small collection of bottles donated to me.

Victorian ice cream moulds from the collection of Emma Kay. (© Emma Kay)

Marshall's food colourings including sap green from the collection of Emma Kay. (© Emma Kay)

Although this was not an unusual recipe for the time, Agnes's inclusion of the additional flavours of cinnamon and bay leaves would have made for a much more exotic and piquant ice cream, compared to the standard formula of apples and lemon, or just apples. The fact that she also uses gelatine, albeit her own brand, to better set some of her iced desserts was also quite unique for a period in history when gelatine powder had only been around for about forty years and the manufacture of it into blocks and sheets was a relatively new concept.

Apple Cream Ice (Crème de Pommes)
Peel and cut up 2 pounds of good cooking apples, put them on the stove in ¾ pint of water, a little piece of cinnamon, the peel of a lemon, the juice of one, 2 bayleaves, 6 ounces of sugar, and 3 sheets of Marshall's gelatine. Cook quickly until reduced to a puree, then pass it through the tammy cloth or hair sieve, and mix it with 1 pint of sweetened cream (No.5) or 1 pint of custard (Nos 1 to 4). Add a few drops of Marshall's sap green. Freeze and serve as for previous recipe. Serve as a dinner or dessert ice.

Brown bread ice cream was a surprisingly popular and commonplace recipe of both the eighteenth and nineteenth centuries, combining brown breadcrumbs, cream, and either sugar or a liqueur, the latter ingredient more of a nineteenth-century adaptation. When recreating Marshall's variation, I used a simple cherry syrup with delicious results.[23]

Recreation of Agnes's apple ice cream. (© Emma Kay)

Brown Bread Ice (Crème de Pain Bis)
Make a pint of brown bread crumbs and mix them with 8 tablespoonfuls of noyeau or maraschino syrup, a few drops of vanilla essence, and 1 pint of cream or unsweetened custard, and freeze dry. Serve in a pile or mould. This is a good entrement or dessert ice, and is much liked for garden and evening parties. It can also be served as a supper ice.[24]

Agnes once again turns to chefs of the past by taking inspiration from several recipes included in William Jeanes's book *Gunter's Modern Confectioner*. As confectioners with royal patronage, Gunter's provided all manner of specialist cakes and sweetmeats to George III and Queen Charlotte. They also made the wedding banquet cakes for Queen Victoria's marriage to Albert, as well as the 'wedding favour' cakes for important guests. By this time, Gunter's had been the bakers, confectioners, and caterers to London's aristocracy and royalty for half a century.

In *Victorian Ices & Ice Cream*, Barbara Ketcham Wheaton accuses Agnes of directly copying a recipe from Jeanes, an employer of Gunter's, although both are very different. The recipe is for Grape Water Ice. The suggestion that it is copied is attributed to neither Jeanes's or Marshall's

Above: Recreation of Agnes's brown bread ice cream. (© Emma Kay)

Right: Recreating Victorian ice creams. (© Emma Kay)

recipes containing grapes. Both include elderflowers. However, a quick search in recipe books of the same era determines that many included elderflowers for making Grape Water Ice, or Ice Grape Water, including the great Frederick Nutt. Jeanes also made his Grape Syrup recipe using elderflowers. So, this was either just a strange unexplained common culinary anomaly, to replace grapes with elderflowers, or plagiarism was so rife that writers copying each other's texts didn't even notice that some recipes that were titled grape didn't actually include grapes.

I am more inclined to go with the former explanation, particularly as the flavour of elderflowers has often been compared to that of grape skins and Agnes, as we know, tried and tested all of her own recipes, so one would expect her to know the difference between cooking with grapes and elderflowers.

Fancy Ices

On publication in 1894, *Fancy Ices* was heralded as one of the best books on the subject ever to be written. Its distinguishing royal blue and silver cover, showing a polar bear standing among icebergs holding a tray of ices, is striking today and must have been hugely appealing back in the nineteenth century. Copies are rare today and can be acquired for a substantial cost. Back in 1894, a copy would still set you back 10s, the purchasing power of which was around £45, for a very slim volume indeed.

Many of the recipes in Marshall's *Fancy Ices* do not appear anywhere else, although the inclusion of some typical Victorian recipes like Belgravia and Duchess Marie biscuits deliver versions far more extravagant than the standard bakery-store goodies of the same name of the time. She created a second volume of ices to include recipes that covered 'more elaborate styles of service'.[25] Marshall is not wrong, as the book contains many of what I would term 'high end' recipes to test even the best of chefs, from challenging baskets of ice mushrooms, constructed from frozen chocolate custard, to complex frozen layered jellies, sophisticated frozen puddings and bombs, even an entire frozen chocolate duck complete with glass eyes, sitting on a nest of spun sugar.

Marshall does, however, provide instructions for making spun sugar, alongside a rather extraordinary illustration of (herself?) carrying out the technique, standing on a chair, throwing a thread of hot sugar over a rolling pin up into the air.

Spun Sugar
Put half a pound of water and one pound of Marshall's Cane Sugar into a clean copper sugar boiler or thick stewpan, cover the pan over, bring the contents to the boil, remove any scum as it rises from time to time, and continue boiling until the liquid forms a thick bubbled appearance (commonly called the crack); then take a small portion on a clean knife or spoon and plunge it immediately into cold water, and if it is then quite brittle and leaves the knife or spoon quite clear it is ready for spinning. If it clings or is all soft or pliable continue the boiling until as above.

When ready, take a small portion on a fork or spoon and rapidly throw it to and from [sic] over a slightly-oiled rolling pin; continue until sufficient threads of sugar are obtained.[26]

Fancy Ices also contains a section on rather random and confusing sundries, supposed accompaniments to frozen dishes and generic cold recipes, ranging from aspic and iced coffee to pastry, icings, and jellies. I can't determine whether Agnes really felt it necessary to include these, ran out of recipes for cold desserts, or simply needed to increase her word count, but this collection of miscellaneous recipes is a little confusing to the overall context of the book. Although, saying that, there was a great deal of fuss placed upon accompanying dishes during the Victorian era, so perhaps it was just pandering to this.

I often get quizzed about the provenance of food and drink and while many exotic products were available from the earliest of times through global trading, which peaked during Roman occupation, it is important to remember that most of these luxury items were only available to a very small percentage of the elite population. Lemons probably first came to the attention of the English during the Crusades, before being imported from Europe during the fifteenth century. Lemon water, or cordial, was extremely popular in the seventeenth century in England and by the nineteenth century, lemons could be found in countless recipes for the middle classes, as a medicinal aid, in pies, marmalade, compotes, fish dishes, and jellies. So it is unsurprising to find a lemon jelly recipe in Marshall's collection. If you

Sugar loaf and nippers from the collection of Emma Kay. (© Emma Kay)

are curious as to what loaf sugar is in this recipe, this was simply the form sugar took before it was processed and mass-produced. A sugar loaf was a lump of sugar shaped in what was often a conical mould, which was broken off into pieces using a pair of sugar nippers before being ground down in a pestle and mortar. Note that the addition of the eggshells helped the jelly set; as a consequence it was very important to sieve your final mix carefully.

Lemon Jelly
For one quart of lemon jelly, peel four lemons very thin, and then cut them in halves, squeeze out the juice, and strain it into a saucepan with half a pound of loaf sugar, a little piece of cinnamon about one inch long crushed up four cloves, and about eight drops of Marshall's Saffron Yellow; break two eggs, put the whites and shells in the pan with the other ingredients, mix together with a whisk, add a quart of hot water and two ounces of Marshall's Finest Leaf Gelatine, put on the stove, and when it boils pass it through a warm wet jelly bag twice or three thrice till clear and when cool add three wineglasses of any liqueur, and use.[27]

It was probably the Romans who introduced raspberries to England and there is certainly an old English word for raspberry bush, a *hindbrer*.[28] Raspberry

Recreation of Agnes's Lemon Jelly.
(© Emma Kay)

Fancy Ices.

syrup and vinegar was undoubtedly a medieval alternative before the arrival of tea, coffee, and chocolate and by the nineteenth century they featured in pies, sauces, compotes, puddings, and jam, as well as being hugely popular in cold dishes, creams, and ices, so it is understandable that Agnes includes raspberries across some twenty recipes in her book of *Fancy Ices*.

> **Raspberry Souffles (Petits Souffles de Framboises)**
> Put into a whipping tin nine raw yolks and three whites of eggs, two ounces of castor sugar, a few drops of Marshall's Carmine, a gill of raspberry puree and a teaspoonful of vanilla essence; whip the mixture over boiling water till it is hot, then remove the pan and continue whipping the mixture till it is cold and thick, and add to it one and a half gills of stiffly-whipped cream, and pour it into some little papered cases. Put these into the charged ice cave for two and a half to three hours, remove the papers, then dish up the cases on a dish paper, sprinkle over the souffles a little finely-shredded pistachio, and serve for a dinner sweet or for dessert with George's Cheltenham Wafers.
>
> Raspberry Puree for Raspberry Souffle. – Take half a pint of freshly gathered ripe raspberries freed from stalks and rub them through a wire sieve and use. When fresh raspberries are not in season, take one and a half tablespoonfuls of bottled raspberries that have been rubbed through a fine wire sieve. The quantities given are sufficient for ten to twelve souffles.[29]

It is in the introduction to this book that Agnes mentions giving her recipes different names to the standard ones that people may have been more familiar with, like dishes on restaurant menus, which perhaps clarifies the difficulty with finding other corresponding versions of her recipes around this era.

Alongside Agnes's European recipes, which are in the main French, Italian, or German, are the American-themed dishes. This could be testament to a time when Anglo-American relations were being firmly re-established in the 1890s, following a century or so of rivalry, as well as a nod to Agnes's time in the United States. Examples include American Bomb, American Cherry Water Ice, American Coffee Ice, American White Currant Cream, Tennis Coffee (American), as well as ices including the Boston Bomb and

Portland Bomb. Famous names also appear with regularity. As a theme which runs through all of her books, we might view these as indicative of Agnes's own influences, her likes and preferences. Ellen Terry Melon pays homage to the leading Victorian English actress, while Lalla Rookh Sorbet references a famous poem of the time. Or was she merely using names that she knew would be familiar to her readers? I would like to think it was probably a bit of both and as such perhaps these names can tell us a little bit more about the everyday woman behind the culinary empire.

A few of the iced desserts included in *Fancy Ices*, like the Nesselrode Pudding, named after the nineteenth-century Russian diplomat, were the creation of other famous chefs. But many, it seems, were christened or re-christened by Agnes herself. If so, we might be led to believe that she admired Marie Antoinette and Lord Nelson, moved in the same circles as the aristocratic Churchill family, enjoyed listening to Puccini's opera, *Tosca*, ate or stayed at the historic and luxurious Midland Grand Hotel, now the site of St Pancras Renaissance, London, visited the Alhambra Palace in Spain, and was familiar with the early Mercedes-Benz automobiles. We know that the Marshalls were keen on their motor cars.

It has been speculated that Marshall was the inventor of the ice cream cone. Certainly there is a recipe for cornet cases, which when served with flavoured iced water or ice cream became 'Margaret Cornets' in *Fancy Ices*, published in 1894. It is far too contentious to claim that this was the first initiative to encase or hold ice cream or a fancy ice. Wafers can be traced back at least to medieval times and it would be obtuse to think that they weren't at some stage used to embrace all manner of sloppy foodstuffs. Italo Marchiony is also credited with inventing ice cream cones while peddling his icy wares on the streets of New York in the 1890s, while the French-American chef Charles Ranhofer included a recipe for thin rolled waffle-cornets filled with a frozen cream of nougat, cherries, and vanilla chocolate pastilles in his classic cookery tome of 1893, *The Epicurean*.[30]

> **Margaret Cornets recipe (Cornets a la Marguerite)**
> Prepare some cornets as below, and just before serving, fill them partly with ginger ice-water (Book of Ices p.26) and partly with apple ice-cream (Book of Ices p.9) frozen quite dry, and dish them up on a paper or napkin. Serve for a dinner sweet or for dessert.

> Cornet Cases – Mix well together half a pound of finely-chopped or ground almonds with four ounces of castor [sic] sugar, and four ounces of fine flour, two whole eggs, a saltspoonful of vanilla essence, and one tablespoonful of orange flower water. Put one or two baking tins into the oven, and when they are quite hot rub them over with white wax, and let the tins get cool; then spread the paste smoothly and thinly over the tins (say one tenth of an inch thick), and bake in the oven for three or four minutes; take out the tins and quickly stamp out the paste with a plain round cutter, about five inches in diameter, and immediately wrap these rounds of paste on the outside of the cornet tins which have been lightly oiled inside and out, pressing the edges well together, so that the paste takes the shape of the cornet, then remove the paste and slip it inside the tin, and put another one of the tins inside the paste, so that it is kept in shape between the two tins; place them in a moderate oven, and let them remain till quite crisp and dry; take them out and remove the tins, and garnet the edges of the cornets with royal icing and blanched and chopped pistachio nuts.[31]

Marshall is also well documented as the first person to write about the use of liquid gas to freeze food. In a 1901 issue of her magazine, *The Table*, she proposed that:

> Liquid air will do wonderful things, but as a table adjunct its powers are astonishing, and persons scientifically inclined may perhaps like to amuse and instruct their friends as well as feed them when they invite them to the house. By the aid of liquid oxygen, for example, each guest at a dinner party may make his or her ice cream at the table by simply stirring with a spoon the ingredients of ice cream to which a few drops of liquid air has been added by the servant; one drop in a glass will more successfully freeze champagne than two or three lumps of ice and in very hot weather butter may be kept in better condition on the table and make milk free from any suspicion of sourness by adding a drop of liquid air to an outer

receptacle into which a jug or butter dish is placed. Liquid air will, in short, do all that ice does in a hundredth part of the time. At picnics it would be invaluable and surely ought to be kept freely on hand in hospitals.[32]

Agnes's inspiration most likely came from the lectures of the Scottish chemist James Dewar, who during the 1890s was wowing London audiences at the Royal Institution with his live experiments, adding liquid nitrogen to water, creating dramatic clouds of fog to prove his point.

Agnes and her husband were very much at the forefront of the advancement of frozen foods and it would have been interesting to see where their innovations extended, if it hadn't been for her untimely death.

Chapter 3

Isabella Beeton

Isabella's journey started some twenty years before Agnes's and despite the way in which we tend to generically lump all sixty-odd years of the Victorian era together as one point of history, it was definitely an age of two halves.

Isabella was actually a baby of the extended Regency generation, the end of the house of Hanover and Georgian rule. Most people associate this era with Jane Austen, fine art, architecture, and elegance. In reality, the sanitary state of London was bad, and waves of cholera washed through districts like Lambeth and Southwark, taking thousands of lives in its swell. Although the working classes weren't all living hand to mouth in derelict conditions, it's unlikely they would have the time or the facilities to keep themselves and their everyday clothes clean. The national economy was stretched, welfare dependency was at a critical level and child labour still integral to society. Nonetheless, glimmers of light pervaded the gloom. Burgeoning rail networks like the Liverpool to Manchester line, which opened in 1830, began to widen communication, trade, and urbanisation. Enclosed ovens were becoming popular (for those who could afford them) and many people were beginning to start their day with a cup of tea and bread, as opposed to beer, spurred on by the work of the Temperance movement and the steady decrease in taxes on food.

By the time Isabella's *Book of Household Management* hit the culinary market, restaurants were beginning to pop up around London offering a more sophisticated alternative to the inns, chop houses, cake shops, and ordinaries. Food was becoming more important, in terms of maintaining a healthy diet and as a necessary means to accommodate the new urban citizen/worker. The poor, however, were increasingly getting poorer and philanthropy was not only essential but thankfully fashionable. The Poor Law was failing and soup kitchens kept many from starvation, while the Ragged Schools attempted to educate children who were born into literally nothing. Benevolent societies were springing up everywhere to help the homeless and destitute, men, women, children all lacking the provisions for basic survival. The literacy levels of men and women overall had increased to around 60 per cent, making books and reading material a popular choice, particularly with the middle classes, eager to better themselves socially.

For many, clothing was rough and food even rougher, and Isabella's love for both fashion and recipes was intrinsic to this era.

Beginnings and family

You might be confused with the wealth of literature associated with Isabella considering she died in 1865: *Beeton's English Woman's Cookery Book, Mrs Beeton's Everyday Cookery, Beeton's Housewife's Treasury of Domestic Information, Mrs Beeton's International Cookery, The Household Encyclopaedia and Practical Home Physician*, to name but a few, all published after her death, mainly in the genres of etiquette, advice, and cookery. She actually only wrote one book and part of another which was just a variation on the first and for this she became one of, if not the best-known female cookery writers of her generation and remains a household name today.

Like Agnes Bertha Marshall, Isabella's father died when she was young, a death which we know was sudden and unexpected, and her mother remarried.[1]

Isabella was born in 1836 at 24 Milk Street, Cheapside, the site of London's medieval milk market since 1140, which had closed by the time Isabella entered the world, becoming restyled as the heart of London's textile industry. This was the home of her father, Benjamin Mayson, a Cumbrian man and linen wholesaler who moved to London sometime around 1820/30, and Isabella's mother, Elizabeth Jerrom, who is listed on her marriage certificate as a 'minor'. This doesn't sound as creepy as it looks. Elizabeth was 20 years old when she married Benjamin, but parental consent was still required for both men and women up to the age of 21. As it is, her father Isaac granted permission, so he must have approved of the match.

Elizabeth Jerrom was the daughter of Mary Standage and Isaac Jerrom, Isabella's maternal grandparents. Originally from Hampshire, Isaac is listed in 1798 as a tenant paying tax on a piece of land in Southampton,

Above: Morley's warehouses, corner of Milk Street, where Isabella was born c.1840.

Left: Elizabeth Jerrom. (Reproduced by permission of Surrey History Centre. Copyright of Surrey History Centre Ref. 4124/2/24 – 'Mrs (Elizabeth) Jerrom'. Lady sitting)

to the Hawleys, a prominent local family who owned a number of estates in Hampshire.[2] It is unknown what he was using this land for but Isaac must have moved to London in his twenties, which is where he married Mary, originally from Sussex, in 1814 and he is listed as a servant, living in Marylebone, three years later.[3]

Isaac kept a Livery Stable in Wyndham mews near Montagu Street between at least 1825 until his death in 1839, aged 55. At the time of his death, he was living in Montagu Mews, Bayswater Square, originally the coach houses accommodating Montagu Square, which was then a newly built garden square of affluent properties and Isaac's place of work for at least fifteen years.[4]

Confirmation of Isaac's occupation as a stable-keeper can be found in the records of the Old Bailey in 1829, when he took Robert Owen, a petty thief, to court for stealing one of his horse collars. Robert was found guilty and Isaac had his collar returned, worth 5 shillings, or around £20 today.[5]

All we can glean from this information is that Isabella's grandfather, like the majority of the labouring classes in nineteenth-century Britain, was a survivor. We know he had some kind of business, most probably

Ford opposite Hays Farm, Hartley Wespall, where Isaac Jerrom rented land. (By Simon Burchell: https://creativecommons.org/licenses/by-sa/4.0/deed.en)

equine-related as a young man in Southampton, before trying his luck, like so many did, seduced by the promise of success in the country's capital. Biographer Kathryn Hughes suggests that his early days were spent working as a domestic servant in London, which is possibly where he met Mary. We know from the record of their son William's birth that this was the profession of at least one of them for a time. It is strange, however, that neither Isaac or Mary appear in any of the census records for 1811, 1821, or 1831. If they were domestic servants, they would have been listed as such in whichever property they were working.

Isaac fought for justice in the courts as a family man, not prepared to lose his hard-earned money, and made an independent living for himself in the burgeoning salubrious community of Marylebone.

Less is known about Mary, Isabella's grandmother, other than that according to Kathryn Hughes she was the daughter of a groom who worked on the Duke of Richmond's estate. But she was heading up part of the Dorling family (the name Isabella inherited when her mother Elizabeth later married Henry Dorling) probably to provide some respite to Elizabeth and Henry, in 1851, living with four of her young grandchildren in Shipborne, Kent: William, Alfred, Francis, and Lucy Dorling, together with a couple of servants to take care of them all.[6]

Isabella's stepfather Henry Dorling and the rest of the Dorling brood had moved out of the Grandstand and into Ormonde House located in what is now Epsom High Street.

Mary died, having been cherished as a loving member of the family at home in 42 Rutland Street, Pimlico in 1873.

It's interesting to think that Isabella's mother Elizabeth fell in love with a man second time around whose life revolved around horses, just as her grandmother Mary had, although the latter courtship was probably due more to circumstances than anything else.

Isabella's paternal grandfather, the Rev. John Mayson, died amongst family in Milk Street aged 83. He appears in the census of 1841, aged 79, living with his granddaughter, 5-year-old Isabella, in the Mayson family seat at Orton, Cumberland. John's wife and both his sons would have been dead and Isabella's grieving mother was busy caring for three babies back in London. It would appear John Mayson was the only person available to care for Isabella at this time while Elizabeth struggled with 18-month-old John and 4-month-old Esther. Being 5 years old, living in rural Cumberland

Right: Mary Jerrom, Isabella's grandmother. (Courtesy of Bourne Hall Museum)

Below: Ormonde House, home of the Dorlings in Epsom, c.1860. (Courtesy of Bourne Hall Museum)

with only a 79-year-old man for company, must have been challenging for Isabella and probably even more challenging for her elderly grandfather.

There were two other people living with Isabella's mother at the property in Milk Street, 15-year-old Jane Woodcock, who is listed later in life as a nurse, and someone called Robert Michell, who was 35 and may possibly have been a lodger. Interestingly, Isabella's sister Elizabeth 'Bessie' Mayson junior was not residing at the property. Presumably she was staying with other family members or friends. Again, one wonders where Isabella's maternal grandparents were at this time. Perhaps they were beholden to employers, living on site somewhere and without the means to offer a place of their own to stay. A 3-year-old Elizabeth Mayson is listed in a house with a random group of residents, mostly family but some not, ranging from coffee house workers, drapers, a waiter, and a jeweller, ages ranging from 15 to 80, with little Elizabeth standing out by name and age at the same time in 1841. The property was number 5 Houndsditch, a notorious slum district. Could this have been Isabella's sister? Being temporarily cared for by a family friend in the dodgy backstreets of East London?

Elizabeth senior must have felt very scared and alone after the death of Benjamin. It's not clear about her financial situation, but many middle-class women were provided for in the nineteenth century from the investments and insurance policies their husbands would have accumulated in life. For most, the best option was to remarry as soon as possible to secure a longer-term reliable future.[7]

Some middle-class widows would have no choice other than to take up employment as a teacher, governess, or nurse, positions which would maintain their status in society, rather than being forced into domestic service or dressmaking. For plenty of women, the workhouse was always just a pay packet or two away from becoming a reality. Lucky for Elizabeth, she still had family alive to support her, which was not always the option in a period when life expectancy for the middle classes was around 50 years of age.

Isabella's paternal grandparents John and Isabella (née Trimble) Mayson were Cumbrian folk who had three children, including Isabella's father Benjamin. Their eldest son John junior, who would have been Isabella's uncle, died following a long illness aged just 24. He is referred to as an amiable and much respected man.[8] Her aunt Esther married a landowner and yeoman, John Burtholme, and it looks like both her and her daughter

Annie farmed the land. The Burtholmes were also able to employ farm hands and domestic staff, so life may have been productive for them.

Rev. John Mayson was a member of the clergy, curate of the village of Thursby near Carlisle for forty years and nineteen years rector of Orton village, Cumbria. This would have been a simple life and it's not hard to see why Isabella's father Benjamin decided to try his luck in London at the forefront of a thriving urban industry. John Mayson was 84 when he died, a great age in 1845. His wife Isabella had not long died when Isabella junior went to live with him in 1841.

Isabella had a sister, Elizabeth (Bettie), and a brother, John. Her father Benjamin died before he witnessed the birth of his final child and Isabella's youngest sister Esther Mayson in 1841. There is a portrait in the National Gallery depicting all the Mayson children as ethereal sprites, painted by Isabella's stepfather Henry Dorling. Central to this picture is Isabella, the eldest child, who stands apart from her siblings as the only one with blonde, as opposed to auburn, hair. Dated 1848, she would have been 12. This is the only known work by Henry, who apparently painted all of his children.

All Saints Church, Orton. (Andrew Bowden https://creativecommons.org/licenses/by-sa/2.0/legalcode.jpg)

Esther Mayson. (Reproduced by permission of Surrey History Centre, Ref. 4124/1/97 – 'Miss (Esther or Bettie) Mayson, Epsom': no. 124)

When Isabella's biological brother John Mayson was aged around 21, he was living in Aldgate, London. I determined from the records that his occupation was something to do with hotels. This is confirmed with an announcement that appeared in *The Sporting Life* of Wednesday, 6 August 1862, detailing John's position as newly appointed manager of the St. Katharine Docks Hotel, along with a letter to his sister Isabella, dated 1863, from the same hotel. John's workplace is documented as providing the catering for race days at the Grand-Stand, Epsom.[9] A little bit of nepotism goes a long way.

It was a luxury hotel with regular guests including the famous Parisian artist Paul Gavarni.[10] Advertisements like the one appealing to 'Gentlemen, Brokers and Captains' to patronise the dining rooms and 'superior accommodation' appeared widely in the Victorian media.[11] To have been manager of such an affluent hotel at the heart of London's bustling sea trading centre must have been quite an achievement for John, who just two

Photograph of Henry Dorling c.1860s.

years earlier was striking out in his new career, living in a boarding house with a family and three servants. The head of the family that John was lodging with was Thomas Gibbons, an outfitter (a tailor or seller of men's clothing) who employed two people in his business. Given the nature of his business, Thomas Gibbson may well have been a friend or business associate of John and Isabella's father, Benjamin.

Corresponding records suggest John Mayson died in 1871, aged just 31. His last known address was 7 Bristol Gardens, London, although this same year he is also listed in the census as being married to Emily Mayson, the daughter of William Holt, a victualler, and the former manager of St Katharine Docks Hotel. In 1871, she was 29 years old and working as a 'Daily Governess'. By this time, John had replaced his role as hotel manager to one of 'gentleman'. Perhaps he married into a fortune or maybe he had even made his own in a short space of time. Emily, registered as a widow, died in 1883 aged 40. It would appear that she and John had twins in 1866, but I can find no further record of them after the initial birth was announced.[12]

Elizabeth (or Bessie) Mayson, Isabella's biological sister, was still living in the family home at age 23 and had no occupation. In fact, Elizabeth died a spinster in 1927 and left her entire estate of just over £1,200 (equivalent to about £50,000) to her sister Esther, also a spinster. The sisters, together with their half-sister Amy Dorling, some twenty years their junior, were living together with a cook and a housemaid at number 31 Elsham Road, London, in 1881. Now, largely converted into flats, these were once very grand 5/8-bedroom terraced houses in the heart of Kensington. The sisters were all employed as assistants – assistants of what, I have no idea.

Amy Dorling. (Reproduced by permission of Surrey History Centre, Ref. 4124/1/46 – 'Miss Amy Dorling, Epsom': no. 58)

As a middle-aged spinster, Elizabeth moved in with Amy (then Richmond) and her new family. It was a busy household with extended family on both sides and at least four servants, located in Myton Road, Dulwich, London. It seems that Elizabeth and Esther reunited as housemates in 1905, living together at 56 Warwick Road, London. Esther died in 1931 and is buried in Epsom Cemetery. Nancy Spain wrote at some length about both Bessie and Esther's dislike of Sam Beeton, Isabella's husband, that they were disparaging of the limited amount of time he spent visiting the family. She also hinted at their dislike of having to care for the younger children in the ever-expanding Dorling brood. Perhaps it was Esther and Bessie's disapproval of Sam, combined with their lack of maternal instincts, raised in a house swarming with childcare responsibilities, that validated their lives of spinsterhood.

As firm family friends, both widow and widower, it was probably inevitable that Isabella's mother Elizabeth Mayson and Henry Dorling would forge a relationship. They initially ran away to Gretna Green in 1843 to marry, before legitimising it again in London several days later. Was this indicative of a fun streak in the couple, or were they trying to avoid something? Henry Dorling was initially a bookseller, then a master printer of race cards who was successful enough to employ several staff once business took off. According to Isabella's biographers Nancy Spain and Kathryn Hughes, Isabella's mother Elizabeth had first fallen in love with Henry when she was a young girl, but her parents had deemed him unsuitable. This may just be conjecture, but we do know that Henry and his first wife Emily named their first child Henry Mayson after Henry's good friend and Isabella's father, Benjamin Mayson.[13]

Henry Dorling became Isabella's stepfather and she inherited a whole new family. A widower, Henry already had a 6-year-old daughter called Jane. At 7, Isabella would most certainly have played together with Jane and her slightly older stepbrothers, Henry Mayson and Edward, while her youngest stepsister Mary was probably ripe for mothering. Isabella's mother Elizabeth gave birth throughout the 1840s to thirteen half-brothers and -sisters to Isabella: Charlotte Emily Dorling, (1843), Helen Dorling (who died at birth in 1845), William George Bentinck Dorling (1846), Alfred Curtiss Dorling (1847), Lucy Dorling (1849), Francis Dorling (1850), Eliza Dorling (1851), Alice Dorling (1853), Edith Harriet Dorling (1854), Walter Dorling (1855), Amy Dorling (1859), Lionel Dorling (1860), and Horace Norman Dorling (1862).

Isabella's mother was only 56 when she died. She had spent virtually her whole adult life pregnant and rearing children.

The family initially lived inside the vast expanse of Epsom Downs grandstand, which Henry leased for £1,000 per annum until around 1851. It seems unthinkable that a grandstand built for thousands of spectators could become a private residence, but the building had already been fully fitted out with kitchens, bedrooms, and living spaces to accommodate Queen Victoria back in 1840.[14]

Henry then occupied his father's previous residence and business premises, Ormonde House in Epsom's station road, now the High Street, which he moved part of the menage into.

The stepfather

Henry Dorling and Samuel Beeton fell out publicly in 1868 over Samuel's publication, *The Sporting Life*, which survived a chequered history of financial uncertainties. In a souvenir publication for the Derby that year titled *London's Great Outing: The Derby Carnival*, Samuel wrote a semi-libellous accusation of Dorling, who it appears may have been an anonymous partner or financial backer for *The Sporting Life*, remarking:

> The Clerk of the Course has studied too closely for one and twenty years the art of filling his pockets from every available source, and is too fond of the red gold not to have made everything that he had any control over quite easy to purchase. Ready, ay, ready to sell anybody or anything, that's the family motto.[15]

This bitter and blatant attack, not only on Henry, but the Dorlings as a family, is affirmation of Samuel's real disdain.

The son of a bookseller working in Epsom, Henry, originally from Ipswich, Suffolk, became a bookseller himself before branching out into printing following a seven-year apprenticeship in London from which he began printing race cards, finally becoming the Clerk of the Course of Epsom Downs after implementing numerous improvements to the course.[16] Henry launched the 'correct card' and introduced the 'preliminary canter' at Epsom race track from 1846 as part of his duties as the first official Clerk of the Course, the person ultimately responsible for the smooth preparation

Sporting Life, 1898.

and management of race meetings. It is said that Henry never placed a bet himself.[17]

Henry was an all-round asset to the community and local commerce, spending some thirty years acting as chairman for the Epsom Local Board of Health. He played five different wind instruments with great skill and is said to have adored children, just as well, considering he had so many of them.[18]

Biographers of Isabella tend to mould Henry into the epitome of fine, gentlemanly Victorian dependability, and maybe he was, but there are examples of him being disliked and mistrusted. He was also petulant. Henry did little to mend the rift between himself and Samuel, in fact he blatantly exasperated it on many occasions. When he noticed that letters being sent from Sam to Isabella had the 'Boy's Own' promotion logo on them, as Sam sent them directly from his office, he fatuously remarked that it was an example of Samuel's flagrant abuse of advertising.[19] Henry was also parodied in an 1841 edition of the satirical magazine *Punch*.

Henry Dorling died at Stroud Green House, Croydon in 1873, two years after his wife Elizabeth. Stroud Green House, built in 1788, now Ashburton

Caricature of Henry Dorling in *Punch*, 1841.

Park, was a vast property standing in many acres of land and Dorling lived there with his family from about 1869, with the help of a butler, footman, groom, cook, lady's maid, several housemaids, and a kitchen maid, as well as a team of gardeners and coachmen who lived in separate properties in the grounds.[20]

Henry left 'effects under £80,000' in his will. So, somewhere in the region of around 5 million pounds in today's spending power. Undeniably he had accumulated considerable wealth in his lifetime.

His legacy lives on in Ewell, near Epsom, where a street, Dorling Drive, was named in the 1960s to commemorate Henry.

Following his father's death, his son Henry Mayson Dorling became 'Clerk of the Course', in addition to Chairman and Joint Managing Director, giving him more control at Epsom. Henry junior was known as 'The Dictator of Epsom Races', a title which left him unfazed, saying, 'Everyone hates me and I like it.'[21]

Maybe these are traits he took from his father Henry, who was undeniably a man combining both charm and fierce ambition.

Isabella's stepfather Henry Dorling is often portrayed as the doting, respectable, and hierarchical lynch-pin of the family, but he was also a capitalist and a man who would have exploited, manipulated, and used ruthless tenacity to get what he wanted. Her husband Samuel didn't like him or what he represented and the feeling was mutual. The opinions of Henry and in turn the rest of the wider Mayson-Dorling family's opinions on Samuel, undoubtedly influenced by Henry, should not shape our own opinions about Isabella's husband.

Henry Mayson Dorling. (Courtesy of Bourne Hall Museum)

The half-siblings

Henry and Isabella's mother Elizabeth's children offer a rich mix of personalities and characters who reflect a great deal about Victorian life and its class culture.

Charlotte Emily Dorling married distinguished army Lieutenant-General Charles Alexander McMahon in 1868. It was McMahon's second marriage. Charlotte gave birth to her first daughter Florence in 1871, who sadly died just two years later. She then had a son, Hubert, who only lived for one month, followed by another son, Hugh, who again only lived for about a month. This was indicative of the age they were born into. Then there was Francis Lionel McMahon, who lived until he was 20, and Edith Beatrice McMahon and Alfred Alexander McMahon, who both lived good lives. All of Charolotte and Charles's children, with the exception of Alfred, were born in India. It seems they returned from India sometime around the late 1870s and by 1891, they were living on the Isle of Wight with 24-year-old Josie McWilliam, Charles's daughter by his first marriage.

Isabella's half-brother William George Bentinck Dorling died in 1880, aged 35, in New Orleans, Louisianna. In 1870, by the age of 24, he had bravely emigrated to the United States and become an editor living in a shared house with a group of bohemian writers and merchants of mixed ages in New York City. William was also the editor of *The American Racing Record and Turf Guide* published in the US.[22] It was a magazine priced at $1, described as:

> Containing a complete digest of all turf events in the United States and the Canadas ... a brief description of each race, with the betting, and an index giving the pedigree of every horse engaged; entries for the stakes ... the winners of the principal races in America and England from their commencement; the racing colors of the leading turfmen; table of the fastest time made at different distances; list of thoroughbred foals.[23]

The *Chicago Daily Tribune* informs us that William, who is cited as also working for *The Sporting Life* in London, was staying at the Sherman House Hotel, Chicago in the spring of 1879, the year before he died.[24] This was one of the city's biggest hotels, which attracted high-profile celebrities and visitors.

William must have been very successful and on close terms with Samuel Beeton and was probably the most adventurous of all Isabella's brothers, although Alfred Curtiss came a close second.

'New world' countries made appealing prospects to young people of the Victorian era, especially those trapped in industry, working in the overcrowded cities with limited opportunities. Alfred Curtiss Dorling was in Australia in 1862 when he died rowing across Hobson's Bay in Melbourne. He was just 15 years old, serving as a midshipman in the Navy. A search for the bodies of Alfred and his three fellow shipmates resulted in the discovery of two bodies 'frightfully mangled', together with a message in a bottle which chillingly read:

> This morning, Sunday, we, four midshipmen from the Dover Castle, hired a boat at Sandridge, and proceeded on a voyage down the bay. Off Brighton we sprung a leak, and do not expect to be afloat five minutes. Anybody finding this will please reveal its contents. Good heavens we are going down.[25]

The following year, Isabella's long-awaited healthy son Orchart Beeton was born. What a bittersweet turn of fate.

Isabella's half-sister Alice Dorling also died young, at 16, while Eliza Dorling married a solicitor, Charles Roberts, moved to Devon and had three children, in what appears to have been a fairly uneventful life.

Lucy Dorling is often allocated the title of Isabella's favourite sister and the one who would help her in the kitchen, despite being twelve years Isabella's junior. Isabella and Samuel's biographer Nancy Spain was Lucy Dorling's granddaughter.

Lucy married William Holmes Smiles in 1874, long after Isabella's death. William was the son of a fairly well-known Victorian, Samuel Smiles, author of a controversial book called *Self-Help*. He is an interesting man, who appears to have failed at medicine, before working at South Eastern Railway for some years, alongside pastimes including journalism and writing. Although it is hard to find much about his son and Lucy's husband William Smiles, other than that he worked in the rope-making business, having such a high-profile character for a father must have made for an interesting upbringing.

Lucy went on to share her mother's love of children, giving birth to eight sons and three daughters in fairly quick succession. The family lived in Northern Ireland, with the help of at least five servants.

Belfast was once home to the largest rope-making industry in the world, so they were clearly in the right place. Lucy lived a good, long life and her legacy lives on as the great-great-grandmother of Edward Michael, or as we know him best, 'Bear' Grylls. [26]

What you might call the middle child, Francis, became a colonel in the British Army and his son Henry Taprell Dorling became an author of some repute, as well as having a notable naval career. Of his younger sisters, Edith Harriet and Amy, the former remained unmarried but was a 'companion' to a slightly older lady called Martha Clayton, while the latter married a colonel, had two sons but was living alone with several servants by 1911.

Walter Dorling was a stock jobber, basically a nineteenth-century term for someone who worked on the stock exchange, and he clearly did well out of it judging from his large estate, The Elms in Horley, complete with five servants.

Above left: William Smiles.

Above right: Walter Dorling. (Courtesy of Bourne Hall Museum)

Henry and Isabella's mother's youngest children Lionel and Horace, both who would have been no more than toddlers when their half-sister Isabella was alive, worked as a colonel in the army and an engineer respectively. Horace's first wife was a drug addict, which eventually killed her; he also had a habit of not paying his bills, if a court case involving debts in 1904 is anything to go by.[27]

We know that of all the siblings, Lionel must have been close to his sister Charlotte, as he is listed as staying with her in South Kensington in the 1911 census.

Isabella's half-brothers were misfits, eccentrics, adventurers, and money-makers, while the most dynamic of all the women in the family was clearly Isabella herself. This may sound a little unjust, given the nature of the world at that time and the limited options available to women generally, but it was also an era of pioneering feminism for the more enterprising women in society. One wonders whether Isabella would have chosen the path she did had she not married Samuel and whether she actually found him more of an attractive option because of this. Goodness knows she'd spent a good enough portion of her youth as a caregiver to many children.

Training and goals

Isabella had received an education at finishing school in Heidelberg, and took subsequent lessons at Barnard's, the bakery and confectioners in Epsom High Street.[28] As a younger girl, she attended Colebrooke House Ladies' School in London at 1 Colebrooke Row, Islington.[29] In 1861, the school was still thriving, specialising in teaching young ladies drawing, singing, and dancing.[30]

William Barnard was a confectioner in Epsom High Street, running a business which was established in 1802. He catered the county balls, local suppers, and wedding breakfasts, with his skills providing 'the liveliest satisfaction'.[31]

By the 1890s, he (ironically) proudly announced that all his cakes were made by machinery.[32] After his death, the premises were converted into tea rooms and renamed Riddingtons. The owners continued to pay homage to Barnard's legacy on the shop frontage.

Barnard's, Epsom, where Isabella trained briefly. (Courtesy of Bourne Hall Museum)

Barnard's when it became Riddington's tea rooms. (Courtesy of Bourne Hall Museum)

It isn't clear exactly what or how William taught Isabella, but as his speciality was making sweets and pastries, it's likely this is what she would have learnt. Pastry cooks in the nineteenth century did not just make what we associate with pastries today – croissants, tarts, éclairs, pain au chocolat, sausage rolls, vol au vents, and so on, they made a wide range of products including puddings, jellies, biscuits, savoury meat patties, fruit and meat pies, cakes and buns, trifles, even ice cream. So it's possible Isabella may have been exposed to a range of skills during her time at Barnard's.

Isabella disliked formal dinners. And she wrote on numerous occasions to Samuel that she found them tedious.[33] Yet in her *Book of Household Management* she declares, 'Dining is the privilege of civilization [while dinner] is a matter of considerable importance; and a well-served table is a striking index of human ingenuity and resource.' Did Isabella even enjoy cooking for others, or did she simply get swept away with the great wave of enthusiasm for it and its commercial value in nineteenth-century Britain?

From everything I have read about Isabella Beeton, it seems that her first love was fashion. She adored clothes, perhaps unsurprising considering the trade of her father; the smell of fabric and machine oil ran in her blood and permeated her early childhood in Milk Street.

Although young women of the Regency and early Victorian era were largely oppressed and resigned to a life of inequality, they did need to marry and marry well. Educational accomplishments were considered trivial, but it certainly helped women to be able to embroider, play a musical instrument, be fluent in different languages, dance, and know how to manage a household. All essential to participating successfully in nineteenth-century society. Private finishing schools were commonplace for wealthy young women looking to complete their education in the Victorian era. The most renowned were in Switzerland, popular for its aesthetic scenery and neutrality, but plenty existed on the continent in Belgium, Paris, and Germany, the latter being where Isabella and her half-sisters studied.

'Miss Heidel's Establishment', located in the quaint fourteenth-century town of the same name in south-west Germany, was also the institution that Samuel Beeton's own half-sisters, Mary Ann (Polly) and Helen, attended. It was undoubtedly the decision of her stepfather, Henry Dorling, to send Isabella to Germany, admiring as he did the customs, culture, and education systems of the country.[34] If he had lived during both world wars, it would have been interesting to see where Henry's loyalties ultimately lay.

Isabella would have learnt the standard dancing, music, domestic economy, needlework, and languages, as well as English and maths. Free time was spent attending balls, nearby historic German monuments, cafés, and going on long walks.[35] There was an English church in Heidelberg and Miss Heidel had a base in London that she used to entertain prospective parents who were looking to send their daughters to the school in Germany.[36]

For about six weeks, Isabella would have been immersed in German culture, while learning to be a better individual, an individual interesting enough to snare a wealthy man.

As much as she praised German yeast, she criticised the country's inferior quality of meat in her *Book of Household Management*. Later editions include chapters on foods from other countries including 'General Observations on French Cookery', Italian, Spanish Indian cookery, and German cookery, among others. Just one example of the many adulterations that have been made to the original volume over the years. If Isabella had originally included a section on German cookery, I wonder what she would have written, given her own experiences. As it is the 1888 version of her book remarks:

> The knowledge of cookery runs through all classes, and is an essential part of a girl's education. German ladies not only give their morning orders to their cook, but personally supervise the preparation of the family meal. Without necessarily themselves putting a hand to the actual cooking, they are careful to watch that ingredients are rightly and properly mixed, and that stove and oven are of the right temperature.[37]

In fact, I wonder who the faces were behind the name of Isabella Beeton, each time the book was modified. Did the publishers consult with cooks and cookery writers? The irony of this extract is the very reason Isabella wrote her book in the first place. There was no formal guidance, no national training centres back in 1861. Europe did not engage in formal culinary training for the masses until the latter part of the 1800s. Anyone reading the later versions of the *Book of Household Management* will have a skewed notion of what culinary learning meant in the decades that Isabella was writing. In his biography, Hyde Montgomery notes that during the Edwardian period, the culinary author Charles Herman Senn edited Beeton's classic book in such a way as to lose her 'characteristic touch'.[38]

Isabella Beeton's *Book of Household Management*, 1901 edition.

Marriage and burgeoning career

Around 1854, Isabella Mayson began a relationship with Samuel Orchart Beeton, the families all having been acquainted for some years. Sam's mother and Isabella's mother in particular had been good friends. Samuel was prolific in the publication of specialist interest and illustrated magazines, while she was a stay-at-home spinster with a brood of siblings to manage. Isabella's life was a catalogue of social obligations and familial formalities, not dissimilar to most women of her age and class in the nineteenth century. They finally married in 1856 and, reading some of the correspondence, it seems incredible that they even married at all. Sam seems to have put as much distance as possible between himself and the Dorlings during their courtship, behaviour that incensed Isabella and her family generally. Samuel's dwindling visits and delayed replies to her letters almost suggest that he was testing Isabella's affections. He was clearly a very busy man about town, chasing business while relentlessly networking. One wonders, however, if Isabella hadn't pursued him as she did with letters and pleas, whether the two of them would ever have actually married; it's as if these lapses in Samuel's reciprocation were at times deliberate. For what reason, though? We know he disliked Isabella's family, particularly Henry, and it's not as if they could have met up in different locations, as this was a time of strict chaperoning. His career was blooming and his free time constrained, or was Samuel pushing Isabella's patience, trifling with her emotions, discerning just how long he could neglect her before she buckled?

Samuel spent six months at one stage dodging the Dorlings. Having spent some weeks sulking over Samuel, overlooking any correspondence, Isabella wrote a blackmailing letter requesting that he collect a parcel for her from London as a ruse to lure him to Epsom, boldly declaring: 'So if you do not make your appearance you will have much to answer for.'

The response from Sam is harsh: 'As I think you will have so much to do, and your house be so pressingling full, I shall not have the pleasure of seeing you next Saturday.'[39]

Each of them is defying the other in some sort of test of will and it seems Sam won out with Isabella, whose upbringing and propriety somewhat subserviently gets the better of her: 'I have been a very cruel, cold, and neglectful naughty girl… begging forgiveness.'[40]

Samuel was back in control and remained so. Had Isabella not made contact, would Samuel have let the relationship run its course? It wouldn't have been at all proper to renounce an engagement, but I somehow think Samuel may not have been concerned with conventions if he really wanted to.

His low tolerance threshold when it came to the noveau riche Dorlings is evident from a letter Sam wrote to Isabella a few weeks before they were married: 'Have father and mamma been using you to-day as of old monarchs used the man who stood behind their chair, ornamented with cap and bells-to-wit-to trot him out, and then laugh at his stepping.'[41]

It must have been very difficult for both Isabella and Samuel, the former remaining loyal to her own loving family, while the latter did his best to disparage and avoid them. The couple's devotion, if that is what it was, somehow invalidated all those issues, marrying as they did in a stressful union.

Sam and Isabella's wedding breakfast was staged in the Epsom Grandstand. Isabella wore 'a white silk dress trimmed with little flounces from waist to hem and a large white bonnet and veil'.[42] One imagines that it was a very stylish dress indeed given Isabella's love of fashion.

Epsom Grandstand, 1830s.

Like Agnes and Alfred, Isabella and Samuel travelled quite extensively, including several trips to Paris. On one such visit in 1860, Isabella reported on the Paris fashion shows in *The Englishwoman's Domestic Magazine*, providing paper patterns, descriptions, and illustrations. This featured as part of her regular monthly column communicating the latest Paris fashions. Isabella began her career in 1857, contributing three monthly articles to her husband's most popular periodical and by 1860, she was editor and resident fashion correspondent.

The Englishwoman's Domestic Magazine launched in 1852, the brainchild of Samuel Beeton. It targeted middle- and lower-middle-class women and was the size of a standard paperback book, with thirty-two pages and a plain cover. Samuel wrote in the first edition: 'The purposes and intentions of our little Magazine are of a nature so different to those of any other now before the public, that we think it necessary to explain at some length the leading features which we intend should characterise it.'

The contents were desirable and accessible, unpretentious, and informative. It also only cost 2 pence. Its reputation as such grew and, according to the *Daily Telegraph*, it had in just one year 'gained a greater number of patrons than any other magazine in the Empire'.[43]

Samuel must in no way be underestimated and written off as the man who was merely the conduit for Isabella's work and one who slowly

1860 fashion plate from the *English Woman's Domestic Magazine*, showing designs by Jules David.

Fashion pages of *English Woman's Domestic Magazine*.

killed her off with a crippling disease. He was a dynamic, hugely prolific, and innovative publisher and journalist on subjects from teenage boys to theatrical books. Some may say a Victorian publishing phenomenon.

By 1856, Isabella had assumed control of the cookery column in Samuel's *Englishwoman's Domestic Magazine*, a prime feature of interest to the growing middle-class audiences of Britain. The majority of these readers did not live in large country estates, or on rural farmsteads, they had moved into the cities to capitalise on the growth and diversity of new industry. Their homes were often smart but cramped terraced houses, perhaps with one domestic servant. Or they invested in the numerous new developments on the outskirts of cities (as both the Beetons and Marshalls did), which frequently entailed long commutes for the head of the household into the city centre. Women who ran these households were struggling with domestic duties. There were no formal cookery schools and cooking and eating revolved around regimental work schedules for many middle-class Victorians.

Prior to 1856, *The Englishwoman's Domestic Magazine* regularly requested its readers to send in their recipes – 'We shall be exceedingly obliged to any lady who will spare a few moments to write out for us some of her choice recipes' – and many others were simply plagiarised from existing books. Not contemporary books either. Researchers of *The Englishwoman's Domestic Magazine* have discovered that the majority of recipes were lifted from cookery books dating to the 1700s and early 1800s, often making them difficult to follow and outdated.

By 1857, Isabella, recognising that the majority of women no longer had the time or the space to grow their own fruit and vegetables and preserve them, or spend hours poring over one dish, felt more comfortable about relying on the slick recipes that were sent into the magazine and she began to update and modernise the cookery column. From this time, it is evident that fewer recipes were being lifted from old books, although many of those old recipes would still make it into the final *Book of Household Management*.[44]

At the height of their successful partnership in 1861, Isabella, then aged 25, and Samuel, 31, were living at 2 Chandos Villas, which used to sit in the county of Middlesex, but is now the London borough of Barnet. Apparently this was later registered as a Pinner address, the same district that Agnes and Alfred Marshall would reside in some thirty years later. The building was destroyed during the Second World War. Obviously

Chandos Villas, Pinner, 1855.

doing well for themselves, they had two servants, Anne and Mary. Their son Samuel had been born and was a year old.[45] They lived at Chandos Villa from 1856 until 1862.

This is the original agent's catalogue description of the Beetons' house in Pinner:

> Chandos Villas
> Lobby and Entrance Hall, Dining Room 16ft. by 16ft. 9in., Drawing Room, 17ft. 6in. by 15ft. 6in., 5 Large Bed Rooms, 2 Water Closets and Domestic Offices.
> Ground 50 feet front, depth 250 feet.
> RENT £50 PER ANN.[46]

Isabella settled into her own domestic life with ease and happiness. There is a report of her engaging with the local community in 1858, by making soup for the impoverished children of Pinner during a particularly harsh winter.[47] And the affectionate correspondence auctioned at Sotheby's in 2011 on domestic subjects between her and Samuel while they prepared the house are touching: 'You wished to know my favourite seeds, I have no partiality for anything particular but, Mignonette, & I think that would look best planted at the edge of the Border…'

These letters from Isabella to Samuel are both full of joyous discussions relating to their new home as well as Isabella's continued concern regarding Samuel's long working hours.[48]

The tenderness that seeps through Samuel's letters to Isabella are testament to his overwhelming grief when, writing in 1864, many years after the loss of one

One of Isabella's favourite border plants – Mignonette.

of their children, he reflects on sharing a room with a baby while staying over at a friend's house: 'Give my best kisses to our dear little pet – one slept in the room last night – and it made my heart ache, you may know – where our first little chappy went away from us. Preserve to us our present joy, and we can bear a good deal of trouble having that.'

Samuel wasn't liked by Isabella's family and he had some questionable characteristics but that isn't enough evidence to discredit Samuel. Maybe he had syphilis, maybe he didn't. If he did, he may very well have been oblivious to it.

Samuel relied on Isabella commercially in many ways; she contributed extensively to his magazines, translated the latest French fashions and cultural intelligence from the continent to inform readers about cutting edge trends. A letter he wrote to her while staying with friends in Newmarket in 1864 denotes this reliance:

> Send the description of the 8 pages you have already got up for the Young E'woman as soon as pos' with the cliches to Cox and Wyman and ask C.W. to let Poulter do the making up, These done, the next thing is the sheet of Dble Demy with 2 sets of diagrams and Needlework patterns, given us, that is to say, the Suppt. For the Y. E'woman for 2 weeks. These two sheets of Dble Demy (the pattern already pasted down and the diagrams as just mentioned) will set us right for 6 weeks. With No. 1 I suppose we had better issue the Patterns and Diagrams 8pp. that is to say N'est-ce-pas?[49]

They were the golden couple of nineteenth-century printed lifestyle journalism, but they worked hard for it.

The children and grandchildren

We know that Isabella suffered multiple miscarriages and two of her children only lived short lives. Her last child would kill her. A great deal has been speculated about this, often attributing Samuel, and his latent syphilis, as the cause. To me, it seems Isabella was just another victim of her time. The 1860s was an era just before the acceptance of the germ theory, and her children, like all others, were born in largely unsanitary conditions, with no antiseptic and no sterilised surgical instruments. Samuel Orchart Beeton was the name bestowed to two of Isabella and Samuel's children and both died in infancy.

Perhaps not wanting to jinx their third-named attempt, Orchart Beeton was born a healthy boy in 1863 and would go on to live a long life. Educated at Marlborough College, he married Janet Kennedy in 1889. Having had a very successful military career, in 1947 Major Orchart Beeton stabbed himself fatally over 300 times with a pair of nail scissors at his home in Worthing. He was 83 years old and a verdict of suicide was given. Orchart was listed as unsound of mind.[50] It was a sad end for a once mighty military man. He was survived by one daughter born in 1890, Iris Beeton, who never knew her grandmother Isabella. Iris Kennedy Beeton married late in life in 1948 to a James John Hone, who died the following year. From census records, it is clear the two had been living together in Finchley

Isabella Beeton, 1860.

for some years and that James was considerably older than her. Iris was a hairdressing assistant. She remarried aged 60 to George Arthur Burnard, thirteen years her junior, who had positions as a draper and a bus driver. Iris died in 1981 age 91.

Sir Mayson Moss Beeton, born 1865, was in possession of all of the letters, manuscripts, and other publications belonging to his parents, who he bequeathed to his grandson Rodney M. B. Levick.[51]

An edition of the *Daily Mail*, 15 November 1947, noted this request, recording what Sir Mayson Moss Beeton stipulated in his will: 'My wish is to preserve intact family records which may be of interest to posterity as throwing some interesting sidelights on the social literary and political life particularly in Victorian and Edwardian periods of English history.'

Like his brother before him, Mayson went to Marlborough College and then onto Magdalen College, Oxford, where he studied history. He spent his life in journalism, writing before becoming president of the Anglo-Newfoundland Development Company.

Sir Mayson Moss Beeton.

He had three daughters and a son with his wife Louie Swinley Price Jones: Marjorie Mayson Beeton, Edith Audrey Mason Beeton, Isabel Cecile Beeton, and William Harmsworth Beeton. Having worked for the *Daily Mail* and as a publisher and author, Mayson Beeton established a timber milling business in Newfoundland, supplying timber for the British War Office during the First World War, for which he gained his knighthood. His daughter Edith Audrey Mayson joined the Red Cross during the war, specialising in massage and electrotherapy. She married the British Antarctic explorer and surgeon George Murray Levick in 1918, who accompanied Robert Falcon Scott on his ill-fated *Terra Nova* expedition. It was during this expedition that Levick documented some of the most important observations of penguin life in the wild.[52]

Of Isabella and Sam's other grandchildren, William was killed in a motorcycle accident in 1914 at just 16 years of age,[53] while Marjorie also served as a voluntary nurse during the First World War, passing an international course of nursing at the University of London. Her husband Leonard Gibbs Kilby was decorated during this war for his service in France.

Dr George Murray Levick sorting a trawl catch.

Post-war life would have offered Isabel Cecile a very different sort of world in which to go forth, compared to her ancestors. She studied at the illustrious Roedean School in Brighton and travelled as an unmarried and unchaperoned tourist to Bombay in 1926 and 1927.[54]

She lived in an elite part of Chertsey with her mother and father in the 1930s before marrying a chartered accountant, Gilbert Stanley Farbrother. Although they didn't have children, they travelled extensively as a couple by ship to Tangier and Indonesia among other exotic locations, before widespread commercial aviation.

Like her namesake, I think Isabel may have had some of the spirit that her grandmother had for travel and independence.

Although they both grew up to be highly respected and successful men in their own right, Isabella and Samuel's boys had a difficult early start in life. Verging on financial ruin and needing a mother figure for his sons, Samuel, Orchart, and Mayson lodged together with family friends Charles Rouse Brown and Matilda Brown, who became the new editor of *The Englishwoman's Domestic Magazine* not long after Isabella died. Charles and Matilda were childless at the time, so they were keen and able to support Samuel and his boys. Samuel's father also had cousins with the surname Brown, so potentially they may have been relations. Sam and Matilda worked closely together, establishing a new popular publication *Myras Journal of Fashion*, which was both written and edited by Matilda. Orchart and Mayson received plenty of maternal affection and a good family life, having had their mother so tragically ripped away from them, while Samuel got his dynamic new editor. It has been intimated that Samuel and Matilda were having an affair, but there is no substance to this, and neither did she die of syphilis-related issues, as one might expect if they had been. In fact, Matilda lived a very full life until she was 99. Charles and Matilda finally managed to have a child together, Charles junior, in 1878, long after Samuel had moved away and died and both boys had flown their adoptive nest. Charles Gordon Brown went on to become a surveyor.[55]

It has been said that Orchart and Mayson never saw the Dorlings, their grandparents, aunts, uncles, or cousins soon after they all moved in with the Browns. It has been suggested that the situation was too scandalous, but it's more likely that Samuel, given that he was no longer obligated and had always detested his in-laws, just made a conscious decision to withdraw his sons from the family altogether.

Samuel Beeton

I think for too long Samuel has been pushed aside in favour of his wife and her death. We forget that he gave Isabella her notoriety, his treadmill of success as a writer and publisher, a cultural and social innovator of the Victorian era who made Isabella Beeton the icon she has become. Without Samuel, I doubt very much that we would ever have heard of Isabella.

In terms of Samuel Beeton's parents, a Helen Orchart married Samuel Powell Beeton in London's Bread Street, 1830, but she was baptised Ellen Orchart in 1808, daughter of Thomas and Mary Orchart. She is then listed in 1832 as Samuel's wife Eleanor on the baptism register for their second son and Samuel's brother William.

William Beeton probably died either at birth or aged 2, as a child born near the same location in the same year, but listed as 'Beaton', can be found in the death register of 1834, a common misspelling. It's also likely given the dates and locations that the name Helen was a moniker for Eleanor and Ellen and they are all one and the same person, with Helen dying around the same time as her second son. Samuel Powell had also remarried by 1834, going on to provide his son Samuel with a further seven half-siblings.

Samuel's father and Isabella's father-in-law Samuel Powell was a warehouseman before becoming proprietor of the Dolphin Arms public house. In the nineteenth century, public houses or inns generally provided food, accommodation, and stabling with the proprietors known as hotel- or inn-keepers, publicans, or, as Samuel Powell was known, a victualler. Despite nineteenth-century inns sometimes gaining a less than salubrious reputation, many were tailored to men and women with high-class tastes and they served an invaluable service to the community, and the Beetons, headed up by Samuel Powell, were a very respected family. He employed some seven members of staff before the pub fell into the hands of his second wife Eliza, until the Beeton ownership was relinquished all together by 1869. The family took one member of their team to court in 1835, when pot-boy James Fitzgerald stole jewellery from Eliza Beeton's bedside drawer. For his crimes, James was transported for seven years.[56]

This exemplifies the harsh realities of nineteenth-century British society and the environment that many were struggling to survive and progress within. Having money helped, but everyone was ultimately walking a precarious line.

Samuel is frequently demonised as a whoring, partying, selfish, and dubious character prior to marriage. Perhaps he was all these things, but he was also jolly clever, a man of his time, self-made and self-assured. He was flawed, addicted to gambling, impulsive, and had I believe a chip on his shoulder, a resentment of others whose money came to them so readily. Above all else, Samuel was an exceptionally hard worker, driven to succeed. He knew the markets to tap into, understood the needs of middle-class women, seeking to advise, befriend, and enrich their minds with his monthly periodical *The Englishwoman's Domestic Magazine*. Again, he recognised a gap in the market with the creation of *The Boy's Own* magazine and the first ever reasonably priced sporting magazine *The Sporting Life*. There is a great deal of criticism about Samuel and his absence from Isabella's side when she needed him, the countless missed family events and gatherings while courting her, his trips away, meetings, and frequent assignations. But Samuel was a workaholic, a relentless grafter whose career depended on networking, building and sustaining relationships, planning, creating, schmoozing, socialising, remaining on-trend. The sheer enormous body of his work is testament to this.

In 1852, Sam had made his fortune going into partnership with Charles C. Clarke, shortly after completing a seven-year apprenticeship at McMurray's paper works. Clarke acquired a pirated version of Harriet Beecher Stow's seminal anti-slavery novel, *Uncle Tom's Cabin*, which, after a slow start, soon made the business a small fortune, due mostly to the fact that the book lacked any conditions of copyright. Rubbing his hands in glee, Beeton used the funds from Beecher Stow's exploitation to start his own business, launching the *Boy's Own Magazine* in 1855. A less documented fact regarding this rather unscrupulous money-making endeavour exists on the part of Samuel himself, who travelled across the Atlantic to present the author with a contribution of £500, a figure which would be worth in excess of £40,000 today. Whether this was commensurate with what he and his partner made from the sales of the book is something we will probably never know. The publicity it generated probably didn't hurt either.[57]

The Boy's Own Magazine was an exceptionally clever periodical which captured an untapped market for 10–18-year-old boys. It has been said by some writers that Samuel invented the concept of the modern teenager by the way he so cleverly interacted with this audience.[58]

The Dorlings, Isabella's stepfamily, and the Beetons had been acquainted for years and both had significant connections with the racing world.

Samuel's father Samuel Powell Beeton ran the notorious tavern and bookmaker's located at 39 Milk Street called The Dolphin. Dubbed 'the Tattersalls of the East End', it was one of the busiest and most successful bookies in London. In 1846, Powell Beeton instigated a partnership with fellow tavern owners to sponsor the Great Metropolitan Handicap race at Epsom that spring. The success of this race grew over the years, expanding into greater ventures, until the Betting House Act prohibited all gambling in public houses in 1853.[59]

Despite their connections, there was undoubtedly tension between the Beetons and the Dorlings. A scathing article appeared in the *Illustrated Sporting News and Theatrical and Musical Review* on Saturday, 7 November 1868, highlighting the long feud between Samuel Powell Beeton and Henry Dorling. The article points the finger at Dorling as a greedy businessman, interested more in money than the sport of racing. It also outlines their mutually beneficial working relationship, propped up by Beeton, despite the 'universal dislike' of Dorling. The writer emphasises the lack of respect for Dorling, who was still alive, compared to the overriding regard the public felt towards the late Samuel Powell Beeton, who established many of the races that Dorling profited from. He achieved this by leasing the ailing Epsom Grandstand in 1845, moving in his monumentally large family and printing business into the building and making improvements to the courses while extending the stand itself. This damning character assignation of Henry Dorling adds further fuel to the argument as to why Samuel spent so much time trying to avoid Isabella's family. Not because he was a playboy rake, but because he simply disliked them.

Brought up surrounded by the exhilarating world of racing, it seemed inevitable that Samuel would be integral to the evolution of the British horse- and dog-racing magazine, *Sporting Life*. He received a substantial share of the business in 1861 and was embroiled in a court case against the original partners which dragged on for several years. In the meantime, Isabella's step-uncle Edward Jonathan Dorling was brought in as managing editor to help turn the paper around. In 1865, Charles Dickens is alleged to have given 'an entertaining, ingenious, and most flattering criticism [of] *The Sporting Life*'. The same year that Samuel reached an agreement in court, before severing all connections with the magazine.[60]

Samuel was an early protagonist for the introduction of paper patterns in dress making. Both he and Isabella spent a lot of time in Paris, feeding back the latest fashion gossip in *The Englishwoman's Domestic Magazine*. In 1860, he included hand-coloured plates designed by the French painter and fashionista Jules David, who was the first man to include contemporary backgrounds within the context of his plates, demonstrating the latest fashions in Paris.

One journalist said of Samuel Beeton: 'Beeton was a man with a genius for starting new projects, but no application to carry them out,'[61] while the Irish politician and journalist T. P. O'Connor defined him as 'A strange, interesting, attractive man'.[62]

All of his big ideas and innovation would eventually amount to very little when, in 1866, Samuel was forced to sell the copyrights, plates, and woodcuts for Isabella's *Book of Household Management*, along with *Beeton's Dictionary of Universal Information, Book of Home Pets, Book of Birds*, and so on, together with other titles that he'd written or owned privately. Despite these sales earning Samuel around £10,000, just two years later he still managed to become bankrupt and was soon living as a lodger with his friends Charles and Matilda Rouse.[63]

Samuel actually died of tuberculosis, aged just 47. Although syphilis is known to hasten the onset of tuberculosis, it was also one of the most common causes of death during the eighteenth and nineteenth centuries, with something like one in seven people contracting it, and it was even worse in densely populated cities such as London. Sam's frequent dark moods, christened by Isabella as 'the miserables',[64] and his ongoing pulmonary issues, coupled with a libidinous adolescence, are not enough evidence to suspect he was infected. In fact, I think Samuel Beeton probably suffered from anxiety and may even have been bipolar with his characteristic

Photograph of Samuel Beeton.

highs and lows, lengthy disappearances, risk taking, and fluctuating fortunes. Respiratory conditions, which is what mostly ailed Samuel, are not commensurate with syphilis, as the disease typically affects the nervous system, prompting headaches, visual problems, dementia, hearing loss, and so on. Pulmonary conditions only occur in late or secondary syphilis, which would have occurred more towards the end of Samuel's life, and even then it is quite rare.[65]

There's a possibility that Samuel's ongoing respiratory problems may also have been related to Autistic disorders, as the two are frequently interlinked, as I know from experience with my own son.

The son of an aspiring middle-class victualler, Samuel was a mix of cockney upstart with a short but strict rural country boys' school education and a traditional apprenticeship.

He elevated himself to the higher-ranking world of journalism, where his creative flair and energy for managing new projects yielded him both success and disappointment. He was clearly an impulsive man, a man of ideas who unfortunately lacked the focus to become a true genius. Isabella must have been excited by these qualities, as equally as she must have been disappointed by Samuel's follies. If she had lived longer, she may have prevented his financial shortcomings, or worse, her stepfather may have stepped in to bridge the financial gap, widening the rift even further between the two sides of the family. This we shall never know.

Isabella suffered enormous personal tragedy, but in the nineteenth century people lived with death every day; it was an accepted reality. Thankfully she never saw the little family that she worked so hard to produce near destitute.

There is no evidence that Isabella died of syphilis-related issues. She died of postpartum complications associated with the streptococcus bacteria following childbirth, and while some have speculated that she had miscarriages and lost children due to transmitting syphilis, it must be emphasised again that during the 1800s infant mortality was extremely high and the reasons could have been numerous. Isabella's half-sister Charlotte also bore several children who only lived for a month or so.

There was barely any mention of Isabella's death in the media. One of the very few references in the *Illustrated Times* in 1865 asserts 'the sudden death of Mrs Isabella Beeton is an event which claims a word of deep regret'.[66]

Portrait of Samuel Beeton, c.1860.

Isabella was a shining product of the Victorian age, harkening from rural working-class stock whose children and grandchildren went on to inherit the fruits of their nascent labours in the thriving, innovative, and economic breadbasket of later nineteenth-century industrial society.

During the 1980s and 1990s, the rights to use Mrs Beeton's name was controlled by several different food firms, Mrs Beeton's Company and Mrs Beeton's Food Ltd, both of which had gone into liquidation by 2014. Perhaps it's finally time to confine these old-fashioned dishes to recipe landfill, to be remembered simply for their nineteenth-century virtues, as it seems the legacy of Isabella and her brief existence far outweighs our affection for the recipes. Or does it…?

Chapter 4

The *Book of Household Management* and Other Stories

The English sociologist and social theorist Harriet Martineau wrote to Isabella Beeton in 1862, sharing her opinions on the *Book of Household Management*. It is one of the few reviews I could source directly from that period that wasn't canvassing or generic newspaper blurb.

> ... It has given me a great deal of pleasure; and my niece, who relieves me of housekeeping, and is a first-rate housewife, declares the book to be very valuable indeed in the cookery part. To us it seems new to state the cost of the dishes, and to the last degree useful. In course of time we shall have gone over a great deal of your ground with much thankfulness to you.
>
> The specifications of the duties of servants are excellent too. The parts we least like are the instructions on manners and in medical matters. Being homeopaths, we think the latter very dangerous – while aware that that part is from a professional hand. I just say this much for honesty's sake, and because I know, from my own experience, that one is glad to hear what people think, when a second edition of one's book may afford an opportunity for reconsideration-whether one remains finally of the same opinion or not.
>
> In nineteen twentieths of the book I think we may delight and rejoice; and I heartily wish you joy of it.[1]

Medications in the Victorian era were limited, with many relying on purging remedies like leeches or rhubarb, or the prospect of curing diseases like tuberculosis with a trip to the seaside. Homeopathy was

The Book of Household Management *and Other Stories*

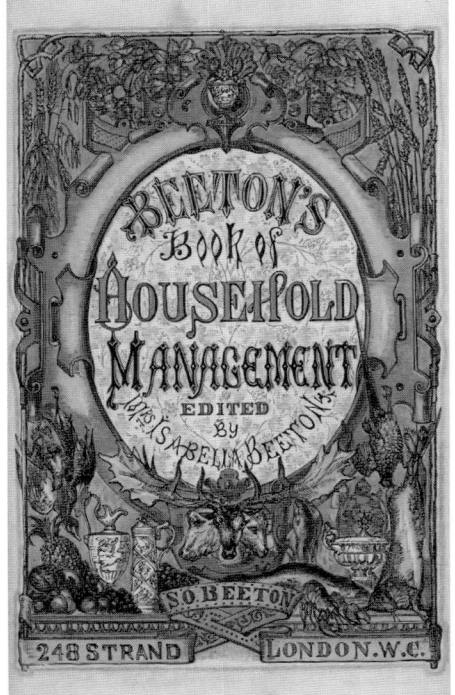 

Above left: Iconic first edition cover of the *Book of Household Management*.

Above right: Photograph of Isabella Beeton aged about 26.

uber-fashionable, endorsed by some of the most eminent people in society, including the Dukes of Cambridge and Northumberland, Earls of Essex, Plymouth, Kinnaird, and so on, lords and ladies a plenty, the list was endless, with the British Homeopathic Society established in London in 1843 as a consequence.

Beeton's 'medical' section to me seems almost entirely reliant on tinctures and herbal teas, but she does talk a little about drugs and pills and the need for doctors (often only afforded by the very wealthy) in a generic way. I can only imagine that Harriet Martineau followed a very strict doctrine that was more medieval than Victorian. She clearly valued the book for its culinary and housekeeping merits and it is clear Isabella must have hit the nail on the head with her whole 'pricing up recipes' notion.

Bits of Beeton

The original version of the *Book of Household Management* was divided into forty-six chapters, containing around 556,000 words, with the cover clearly stating: 'Edited by Mrs Isabella Beeton' and she is humble enough at the start of her most celebrated *Book of Household Management* to indicate that she is 'indebted, in some measure, to many correspondents of *The English Woman's Domestic Magazine*, who have obligingly placed at my disposal their formulae for many original preparations. A large private circle has also rendered me considerable service.'

The English Woman's Domestic Magazine was a popular periodical edited together by Samuel and Isabella and her introduction to *Household Management* is a rather roundabout way of saying that the majority of the recipes were gifted to her by the army of women who submitted them. Bear in mind that the plagiarism of cookery books was rife in the 1800s and had been for centuries, but this somehow still doesn't resonate in an era when many cooks, like Marie-Antoine Carême, William Kitchiner, Alexis Soyer, and of course Agnes Bertha Marshall were also showcasing their own original creations. Beeton does, however, credit some of her recipes directly, most notably to Alexis Soyer, Eliza Acton, Brillat Savarin, Frederick Marryat, William Yarrell, Louis-Eustache Ude, and William Cobbett, and notes that the Bengal mango chutney included in the book was 'given by a native to an English lady, who had long been a resident in India, and who, since her return to her native country, has become quite celebrated amongst her friends for the excellence of this Eastern relish',[2] while the Rev. Sydney Smith, described as 'the witty canon of St. Paul's', known for his love of food and joie de vivre, contributed a salad recipe. Then there are recipes described only as 'given by an intimate friend', or 'a lady from Sussex'. Had the owners of these recipes wanted to remain anonymous or were they just not well known enough in society for Isabella to name them? Perhaps she actually forgot who they were. It seems a shame that so many people contributed to this book, but only distinguished chefs of the time were identified by name.

In *Household Management*, Beeton refers to someone called M. Curmer as 'one of the latest writers of the culinary art'. I have been unable to trace anyone of that name writing in that field in the nineteenth century. There was however a rather influential publisher, L. Cumer [sic], who published a book titled *Le Cuisinier et le Médecin et le Médecin et le Cuisinier ou le Cuisinier Médecin et le Médecin Cuisinier ou l'Art de conserver ou de rétablir sa santé par une alimentation convenable*, or *The Cook and the Doctor and the Doctor and the Cook or the Cook Doctor and the Doctor Cook or the Art of Preserving or Restoring One's Health by a Suitable Diet*. This was an era known for its ridiculously long titles. However, the book was written by someone called Lombard, although it certainly sits in the right period, being published in the 1850s and possessing a vaguely scientific culinary content, which Beeton refers to. She rather humorously derides Curmer as being deluded over his opinion of English beef and its inferiority to French beef. This is also indicative of a time when, despite the fashion for French cuisine, many people across all classes were quick to criticise the French for their influences on English culture. The Napoleonic Wars were not such a distant memory. This quip, even if Isabella did indeed get confused about her authors, was pertinent to the overall national feeling at the time.

The *Book of Household Management* is full of examples of nineteenth-century social commentary, from the warnings about 'dishonest dealers' of meat who relentlessly tried to pass horse tongue off as ox, to Beeton's abhorrence of slavery in Africa, describing it as 'human misery'.

Today's ethical attitudes towards animal cruelty were clearly also at the forefront of Victorian principles, as Isabella notes that the long-standing tradition of brutally slow bleeding calves to produce white veal was all but abolished by 1861. She even remarks on the practice of force-feeding capons that have been 'crammed', instead of being 'naturally fed', the results of which, she bitterly assures, will lead to 'a drippingpan-ful of fat tears', a consequence of the bird's barbarous treatment. These pointed references also provide us with a sense of Beeton's own moral stance. We see flashes of this again in the legal advice section of the *Book of Household Management*, with Isabella affirming 'the law does not this day admit the ancient principle of allowing moderate correction by a husband upon the person of his wife. Although this is said to have been anciently limited to the use of "a stick not bigger than the thumb". This barbarity is now altogether exploded.' This may seem like an obvious illegal atrocity, but the Victorian age was very much entrenched in strict belief systems, the subservience and control of women and the dominance of men throughout all aspects of society. While Isabella is acknowledging the abhorrence of abuse, she also felt it necessary to include this fact for the benefit of her readers, to remind them of their rights.

Isabella's moral stance on animal cruelty also reflects the growing rise of the meat-free movement in the 1800s and the establishment of the Vegetarian Society in 1847. Endorsed by celebrities such as George Bernard Shaw and Isaac Pitman, it became very fashionable to dine out in vegetarian restaurants, to learn how to cook meals without meat and even adopt a healthier lifestyle based on beliefs that vegetarianism could prevent cancer, tuberculosis, and even cholera.[3]

The following is a carrot recipe Isabella included in the book. There are also recipes for carrot jam, stewed carrot, and carrot soup, in addition to one of her – what I call – little asides on the history and varieties of carrot, noting that it was once so highly esteemed during the first Elizabethan era that 'ladies wore leaves of it in their head-dresses'.[4] Note that this somewhat fails as a vegetarian option, considering the addition of suet.

Baked or Boiled Carrot Pudding

Ingredients – ½ lb. of bread crumbs, 4oz. of suet, ¼ lb of stoned raisins, ¾ lb. of carrot, ¼ lb. of currants, 3oz. of sugar, 3 eggs, milk, ¼ nutmeg.

Mode. – Boil the carrots until tender enough to mash to a pulp; add the remaining ingredients, and moisten with sufficient milk to the pudding of the consistency of thick batter. If to be boiled, put the mixture into a buttered basin, tie it down with a cloth, and boil for 2 ½ hours: if to be baked, put it into a pie dish, and bake for nearly an hour; turn it out of the dish, strew sifted sugar over it, and serve.

Time. – 2 ½ hours to boil; 1 hour to bake. Average cost, 1s.2d.

Sufficient for 5 or 6 persons.
Seasonable from September to March.[5]

The few recipes that belong to Beeton herself are credited as 'Author's Recipe'. These include Leamington Sauce, a sort of walnut ketchup, a recipe to make sausages, and Baroness Pudding, which is a basic raisin and suet creation, which Beeton notes was actually given to her originally by a friend who was also a Baroness and an 'Epsom Grand-Stand recipe', which I can

Recreation of Carrot Pudding.
(© Emma Kay)

only assume is a family dish crafted at Isabella's family Epsom estate. Isabella also cites a recipe which she hasn't actually tested herself, for An Excellent Pickle.

Leamington Sauce was a successful commercial sauce, manufactured by several companies in the mid-nineteenth century. George Cundall is understood to be the originator and 'sole proprietor' of Leamington Sauce, which he sold from his Tea, Grocery, and Italian Warehouse in the town of the same name. It is a sauce which was 'respectfully recommended to the nobility and the public generally, as being particularly adapted for every description of fish, Game, Wild Fowl, and poultry. It is also most excellent in enriching Turtle Soup, and for browning in other Soups and Gravies, made dishes, meat pies, maintenon cutlets, hashed venison, etc.'[6] So, Beeton's recipe was merely a version of this existing popular sauce. Her recipe is also reproduced verbatim in countless other books, along with many of the recipes in *Book of Household Management*, which publishers Ward Lock & Tyler attributed to Isabella Beeton years after her death, including *The Englishwoman's Cookery Book*, *How to Dine*, *Dinners and Dining*, *How to Manage House, Servants, and Children*, and so on.

Leamington Sauce

Ingredients – Walnuts. To each quart of walnut-juice allow 3 quarts of vinegar, 1 pint of Indian soy, 1oz. of cayenne, 2oz. of shallots. ¾ oz of garlic, ½ pint of port wine.

Mode – Be very particular in choosing the walnuts as soon as they appear in the market; for they are more easily bruised before they become hard and shelled. Pound them in a mortar to a pulp, strew sone salt over them, and let them remain thus for two or three days, occasionally stirring and moving them about. Press out the juice, and to each quart of walnut-liquor allow the above proportion of vinegar, soy, cayenne, shallots, garlic, and port wine. Pound each ingredient separately in a mortar, then mix them well together, and store away for use in small bottles. The corks should be well sealed.

Seasonable – This sauce should be made as soon as walnuts are obtainable, from the beginning of the middle of July.[7]

Disappointingly, Isabella's sausage recipe is just an Oxford sausage recipe, traditionally made using pork and veal and hugely popular during the eighteenth century. Beeton is often credited with reviving this style of sausage again for the nineteenth century, but recipes for Oxford sausages, very similar to the one Beeton included in her book, were published widely throughout the 1800s before the *Book of Household Management* and can be found, to name a few examples, in *The New London Cookery and Complete Domestic Guide* (1827), *Two Thousand Five Hundred Practical Recipes in Family Cookery* (1837), *Cottage Comforts, with Hints for Promoting Them* (1841), and most notably in Maria Rundell's very successful *A New System of Domestic Cookery* (1805), which, like Mrs Beeton's *Book of Household Management*, was republished in countless new editions. Rundell attributes Mrs Spradbury/Spreadbury to her Oxford sausage recipe, the lady frequently credited with their invention. Spreadbury's epitaph reads:

> Here deep in the dust, the mouldy old crust
> Of Doll Spreadbury lately was shoven;
> She was skilled in the arts of pies, puddings, and tarts,
> And knew every use of the oven.
> When she'd lived long enough, she made her last puff,
> A puff by her husband much praised;
> Now here she doth lie, and makes a dirt pie,
> In hopes that her crust will be raised.[8]

Adding weight to this narrative is an advertisement in the *Oxford Journal* of 1828 informing the public that the sausage maker Mr T. Davis, located in the High Street, Oxford, was the grandson of the sausage maker once apprenticed to a Mr Ben Tyrell, the successor of Dorothy Spreadbury, who invented the Oxford sausage.[9] Here is Isabella's version:

To Make Sausages (Author's Oxford Recipe)

Ingredients – 1lb. of pork, fat and lean, without skin or gristle; 1lb. of lean veal, 1lb of beef suet, ½ lb.of bread crumbs, the rind of ½ lemon, 1 small nutmeg, 6 sage leaves, 1 teaspoonful of savory, ½ teaspoonful of marjoram.

Mode – Chop the pork, veal, and suet finely together, add the breadcrumbs, lemon-peel (which should be well minced), and a small nutmeg grated. Wash and chop the sage leaves very finely; add these with the remaining ingredients to the sausage-meat, and when thoroughly mixed, either put the meat into skins, or, when wanted for table, form it into little cakes, which should be floured and fried.[10]

So, why did the *Book of Household Management* become so popular? Well, timing I think was one significant element, published as it was right in the middle of the industrial revolution when migrating rural settlers found themselves living and working in burgeoning cities, earning more money, and having greater ownership and control of their lives. Women needed to comprehend the basic principles of cooking, whether they were attempting it themselves or hiring staff to do a good job. Unlike the

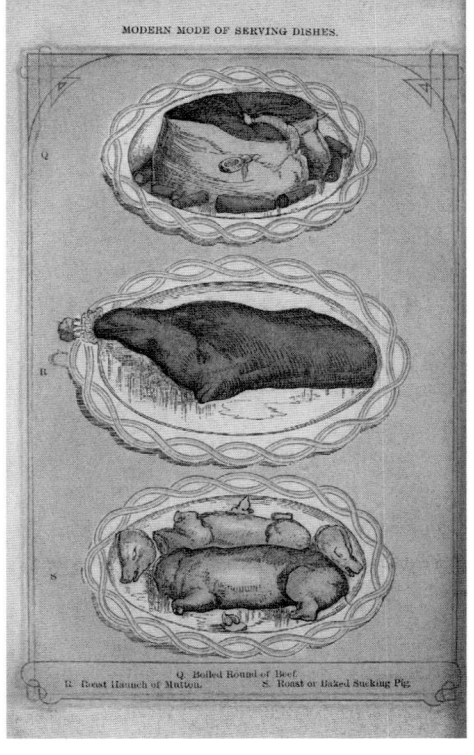

Illustration of Beef, Mutton and Pork from the *Book of Household Management.*

gentry, many middle-class households would often only have one servant who would need support from the mistress of the house, a mistress who would certainly need a good grasp of what was fashionable to cook and serve. Beeton also created the ultimate all-in-one guide containing a wealth of information about everything that was needed to manage a successful household in one handy book, from how to soothe basic ailments, what to wear, how to make and receive social visits, to dining etiquette and the job descriptions of domestic staff, written in a style which was accessible, engaging, and most importantly that placed women at the heart of its focus. In fact, for a book that spans well over 1,000 pages, less than half of those are made up of actual recipes.

What I also like about Beeton's book is her occasional nod to poetry and prose throughout, reproducing quirky and insightful extracts which describe dinner parties or meals. These literary references extend to Lord Byron's observations of a dinner given by Lord and Lady Amundeville, in his poem *Don Juan*, where he rather enthusiastically describes:

> Their table was a board to tempt even ghosts
> To pass the Styx for more substantial feats.
> I will not dwell upon ragouts or roasts,
> Albeit all human history attests
> That happiness for man-the hungry sinner!-
> Since Eve at apples, much depends on dinner.

And from John Keats's *The Eve of St Agnes*:

> While he, from forth the closet, brought a heap
> Of candied apple, quince, and plum, and gourd;
> With jellies smoother than the creamy curd ,
> And lucent syrups tinct with cinnamon;
> Manna and dates, in argosy transferr'd
> From Fez; and spiced dainties, every one.
> From silken Samarcand to cedar'd Lebanon.[11]

These extracts resonate with many prose and poetry entries published in *The Englishwoman's Domestic Magazine*, which may have inspired Isabella to include them in her household manual.

The Book of Household Management *is* skilled in the art of interpreting cooking procedures and techniques while adding clarity to the ingredients themselves, with her little asides. Like the information provided about raisins preceding Beeton's recipe for that most staple of Victorian dishes, the Christmas Plum-Pudding:

> Raisins are grapes, prepared by suffering them to remain on the vine until they are perfectly ripe, and then drying them in the sun or by the heat of an oven. The sun-dried grapes are sweet, the oven-dried of an acid flavour. The common way of drying grapes for raisins is to tie two or three bunches of them together, whilst yet on the vine, and dip them into hot lixivium of wood-ashes mixed with a little of the oil of olives; this disposes them to shrink and wrinkle, after which they are left on the vine three or four days, separated, on sticks in a horizontal situation, and then dried in the sun at leisure, after being cut from the tree.[12]

I have, in my work, been asked many times about raisins, currants, and sultanas, so this is not such a frivolous explanation as it at first may seem. Once a luxury item, raisins were first imported from Turkey and Iran before being sold by costermongers on the English city streets in the nineteenth century.

Again, Beeton's explanation of how to prepare preserved ginger, describing how its long journey from the West Indies was soon to become obsolete, as cultivators in Edinburgh had been able to successfully replicate the West Indian variety, provides a little historical gem.[13] She teaches her readers everything from the cultivation of truffles to the delights of Asparagus Island in Cornwall. Isabella's insightful asides add context to both ingredients and the period itself, making this book something greater than just a compilation of household necessities.

She says of the cucumber:

> Like the melon, it was originally brought from Asia by the Romans, and in the 14th century it was common in England, although, in the time of the wars of 'the Roses,' it seems no longer to have been cultivated. It is a cold food, and of difficult digestion when eaten raw. As a preserved sweetmeat, however, it is esteemed one of the most agreeable.[14]

We know now that cucumbers are excellent for the digestive system, which, along with many other discrepancies, exposes some of the outmoded aspects of the book; that wild boar are extinct in the British Isles, cholera can be cured with a tincture of cinnamon-water and chalk, and that sugar is adulterated with sand and sawdust (although it most probably was then).

This extends to the recipes themselves of course, many of which are fairly obsolete today.

Forgotten favourites

Cabinet, Chancellor's, or even Newcastle Pudding, as it was sometimes called, is now almost completely unknown to the average household, but it was once a cherished variation of bread-and-butter pudding and a favourite of the Regency and Victorian eras. One of the earliest recipes I could find appears in a Swedish recipe book from 1808. Despite its grand name, it is clearly a pudding comprised of leftovers and one that sustained popularity into the 1950s. Cabinet pudding is also very similar to the French dessert, Diplomat Pudding, which utilises sponge fingers or stale brioche. This pudding has a later patronage, not appearing in print until the late 1800s. Diplomat pudding, however, had earlier incarnations as a Diplomatic or even Royal Diplomatic pudding, both of which are jelly based, as opposed to a milky custard. Whatever its origins, during Mrs Beeton's lifetime it was 'very common at fashionable tables, [where] you rarely go to a good and "set dinner" without seeing one'.[15]

> **Cabinet or Chancellor's Pudding**
> Ingredients – 1 ½ oz. of candied peel, 4oz. of currants, 4 dozen sultanas, a few slices of Savoy cake, sponge cake, a French roll, 4 eggs, 1 pint of milk, grated lemon-rind, ¼ nutmeg, 3 tablespoons of sugar.
>
> *Mode.* – Melt some butter to a paste, and with it, well grease the mould or basin in which the pudding is to be boiled, taking care that it is buttered in every part. Cut the peel into thin slices, and place these in a fanciful device at the bottom of the mould, and fill in the spaces between with currants and sultanas; then

add a few slices of sponge cake or French roll; drop a few drops of melted butter on these, and between each layer sprinkle a few currants. Proceed in this manner until the mould is nearly full; then flavour the milk with nutmeg and grated lemon-rind; add the sugar, and stir to this the eggs, which should be well beaten. Beat this mixture for a few minutes; then strain it into the mould, which should be quite full; tie a piece of buttered paper over it, and let it stand for 2 hours; then tie it down with a cloth, put it into boiling water, and let it boil slowly for 1 hour. In taking it up, let it stand for a minute or two before the cloth is removed; then quickly turn it out of the mould or basin, and serve with sweet sauce separately. The flavouring of this pudding may be varied by substituting for the lemon-rind essence of vanilla or bitter almonds; and it may be made richer by using cream; but this is not at all necessary.

Time. – 1 hour. Average cost, 1s.3d.
Sufficient for 5 or 6 persons. *Seasonable* at any time.

Jelly is another dwindling dish, which you are unlikely to find anywhere other than at a children's birthday party these days, or as a foundation for other sweet dishes such as trifles. Savoury jellies are even less popular, aside from aspic. As a unique way to use leftover meat cuts, the calf's foot also proved to be an excellent gelling agent. Once eaten in the coffee houses of the eighteenth century, or as a household restorative medicine/cold dessert, it is a dish you will find in just about every recipe book in the nineteenth century, although its origins are rooted in the later medieval period, once known as 'crystall gelly', as with Hugh Plat's recipe in his *Delightes for Ladies*, published in 1609, where the broth from the calves' feet was added to ginger, pepper, cloves, nutmeg, musk, sugar, and rose water. Here is the recipe that was included in Beeton's *Book of Household Management*. It includes isinglass and eggshells, which were both commonly used as setting agents, the former derived from the bladders of sturgeon.

Calf's feet Jelly
Ingredients. – 1 quart of calf's feet stock No.1411, 1/2lb.of sugar, ½ pint of sherry, 1 glass of brandy, the shells and whites of 5 eggs, the rind and juice of 2 lemons, ½ oz. of isinglass.

Beeton opens the method by asking the reader to refer back to a previous recipe for calf's feet stock. This basically involved scalding the hair off the calf's feet, splitting them in two, removing the fat, boiling them in cold water for around seven hours, and skimming off the fat and sediment. She then instructs to:

> Put it into a saucepan, cold, without clarifying it; add the remaining ingredients, and stir them well together before the saucepan is placed on the fire.
>
> Then simmer the mixture gently for ¼ hour, but do not stir it after it begins to warm. Throw in a teacupful of cold water, boil for another 5 minutes, and keep the saucepan covered by the side of the fire for about ½ hour, but do not let it boil again. In simmering, the head or scum may be carefully removed as it rises; but particular attention must be given to the jelly, that it be not stirred in the slightest degree after it is heated. The isinglass should be added when the jelly begins to boil, this assists to clear it, and makes it firmer for turning out. Wring out a jelly-bag in hot water; fasten it onto a stand, or the back of a chair; place it near the fire with a basin underneath it, and run the jelly through it. Should it not be perfectly clear the first time, repeat the process until the desired brilliancy is obtained. Soak the moulds in water, drain them for half a second, pour in the jelly, and put it in a cool place to set. If ice is at hand, surround the moulds with it, and the jelly will set sooner, and be firmer when turned out. In summer it is necessary to have an ice to put the moulds, or the cook will be, very likely, disappointed, by her jellies being in too liquid a state to turn out properly, unless a great deal of isinglass is used. When wanted for table, dip the moulds in hot water for a minute, wipe the outside with a cloth, lay a dish on top of the mould, turn it quickly over, and the jelly should slip out easily. It is sometimes served broken into square lumps, and piled high in glasses.[17]

A prized platter of the Victorian age, with its origins established in the 1700s and one most people certainly would not indulge in today, was turtle soup, a dish that was widely imitated as 'mock turtle soup' due to the dwindling number of green turtles – a consequence of both its popularity and its expense. Isabella writes at some length about turtles, citing turtle soup as the most expensive soup of the century, with the cost of these marine reptiles ranging anywhere between 8d and 2s per lb, or approximately £3–10 today. With an average adult turtle weighing about 3–400 lbs, you can glean the expense. Beeton informs us that England used to import the turtle from the West Indies, for 'the delicious quality of its flesh'. She also mentions the canned variety, which was sold either with or without the fat, the most coveted part of the turtle.[18]

Mock turtle soup was typically made from a calf's head, boiled together with all manner of herbs, spices, and flavourings, bulked out with forcemeat, and is a dish that eventually became more popular than turtle soup.

It was common to serve turtle soup with quenelles, egg-shaped garnishes formed from binding pounded down meat or fish with breadcrumbs, spices, and eggs. This is definitely something you wouldn't find on a menu today, unless you were dining at a traditional restaurant serving haute cuisine. Interestingly, Agnes Bertha Marshall suggests using bouche cup moulds, a sort of much wider and shorter standard bombe mould, nothing like an egg shape, to set her quenelles.[19] It was generally considered usual to mould the quenelles using an oval tablespoon or roll them into shape. The renowned French chef Jules Gouffe used a paper funnel as a makeshift mould, emphasising that quenelles should never be bigger than a small olive.[20] The following is the recipe included in the *Book of Household Management*. These quenelles are designed to represent the eggs of the turtle, which would have been about the size of a ping-pong ball.

Quenelles a Tortue

Take out the fleshy part of a leg of veal, about 1lb., scrape off all the meat, without leaving any sinews or fat, and soak in milk about the same quantity of crumbs of bread. When the bread is well soaked, squeeze it, and put it into a mortar, with the veal, a small quantity of calf's udder, a little butter, the yolks of 4 eggs, boiled hard, a little cayenne pepper, salt, and spices, and pound the whole very fine; then thicken the mixture with 2 whole eggs, and the yolk of another. Next try this *farce* or stuffing in boiling-hot water, to ascertain its consistency: if it is too thin, add the yolk of an egg. When the *farce* is perfected, take half of it, and put into it some chopped parsley. Let the whole cool, in order to roll it of the size of the yolk of an egg; poach it in salt and boiling water, and when very hard, drain on a sieve, and put it into the turtle.[21]

Lark pie, with its vestiges of crude medieval fare, is also a dish most people would be unlikely to sample today. Killing wild birds for their meat is in the main illegal in the twenty-first century, although licences are issued where birds need to be culled as a consequence of disease or over-population. Game birds, of course, come with their own set of regulations.

A strange phenomenon occurred in Teignmouth, Devon in 1820, when the sky became clouded with a flight of larks flying from the opposite side of the coast; many of the birds died, dropping from the sky and drowning, while others were shot, several hundred in fact, by bird-hungry gun carriers. There were so many dead birds that observers commented on the large baskets seen being carried around filled with larks for sale, while the town's bakers' ovens were crammed with lark pies the following day, such was the demand for this dish.[22]

Lark Pie
Ingredients – A few thin slices of beef, the same of bacon, 9 larks, flour; for stuffing, 1 teacupful of bread crumbs, ½ teaspoonful of minced lemon-peel, 1 teaspoonful of minced parsley, 1 egg, salt and pepper to taste, 1 teaspoonful of chopped shallot, ½ pint of weak stock or water, puff-paste.
Mode – Make a stuffing of bread crumbs, minced lemon-peel, parsley, and the yolk of an egg, all of which should be well mixed together; roll the larks in flour, and stuff them. Line the bottom of a pie-dish with a few slices of beef and bacon; over these place the larks, and season with salt, pepper, minced parsley, and chopped shallot, in the above proportion. Pour in the stock or water, cover with crust, and bake for an hour in a moderate oven. During the time the pie is baking, shake it 2 or 3 times, to assist in thickening the gravy, and serve very hot.[23]

Another unfashionable dish, sheep's brains, remained on the menu, both domestic and commercial, as late as the 1970s and 1980s, but it is not a dish you are likely to see served up in many venues in England today. In the Victorian era, however, sheep's brains were at the height of their popularity. Matelote sauce was a popular pairing with fish in the nineteenth century such as pike, trout, salmon, and eel. The celebrity chef Alexis Soyer mentions it frequently throughout his works of cookery. I have included one of his recipes following on from Isabella's preparation of sheep's brains in matelote sauce below.

Sheep's Brains, En Matelote (an entrée)
Ingredients. – 6 sheep's brains, vinegar, salt, a few slices of bacon, 1 small onion, 2 clove3s, a small bunch of parsley, sufficient stock or weak broth to cover the brains, 1 tablespoonful of lemon juice, matelote sauce.

Mode. – Detach the brains from the heads without breaking them, and put them into a pan of warm water; remove the skin, and let them remain for two hours. Have ready a saucepan of boiling water, add a little vinegar and salt, and put in the brains. When they are quite firm, take them out and put them into very cold water. Place 2 or 3 slices of bacon in a stewpan, put in the brains, the onion stuck with 2 cloves, the parsley, and a good seasoning of pepper and salt; cover with stock, or weak broth, and boil them gently for about 25 minutes. Have ready some croutons; arrange these in the dish alternately with the brains, and cover with a matelote sauce…

Time. – 25 minutes. Average cost, 1s. 6d.

Sufficient for 6 persons.
Seasonable at any time.[24]

Matelote Sauce. – For about a pound-slice of salmon make the following quantity of sauce: peel thirty button onions, and put half a teaspoonful of sugar in a quart-size stew-pan, place it over a sharp fire, and when melted and getting brown, add a piece of butter (the size of two walnuts) and the onions, toss them over now and then until rather brown, then add a glass of sherry, let it boil, then add half a pint of brown sauce, and a gill of broth, simmer at the corner of the fire until the onions are quite tender, skim it well, and add a few mushrooms, if handy, season with a little salt and sugar, and sauce over any kind of fish where described. The addition of a teaspoonful of essence of anchovies is an improvement. Use where directed.[25]

A well-documented Victorian practice of replacing the skimmed cream from the top of the milk with sheep or calf's brains is not so unusual as you may think. This was an era racked by adulteration and trickery to reduce costs. The texture of the brains probably added a density to the milk, making it appear creamy, after the cream was removed and sold separately or used to make other profitable products. Brains were affordable, flavoursome, a great source of protein and abundant. Outbreaks of diseases such as BSE in the latter part of the twentieth century led to discoveries in links between the consumption of certain animal products and the transmission of fatal infections, which is ultimately why eating brains fell out of fashion.

British staple dishes

What of the recipes that have stood the test of time, the dining table staples that continue to be enjoyed today? Did Beeton's compendium leave a lasting culinary legacy?

As Isabella reminds us, roast beef has long been a national dish. Although Yorkshire pudding was paired with it in the nineteenth century, as Beeton informs us with her recommended bills of fare (menus) for 'plain family dinners', having roast potatoes as part of a roast dinner is more of a modern concept. In fact, Beeton does not include any recipes for roasting potatoes in her famous book, all potatoes are fried, mashed, Potatoes a la Maître D'Hôtel (boiled and seasoned with dill and butter), baked, boiled, pureed, or steamed. While it is evident in nineteenth-century American recipe books that roast potatoes and roasted meats were combined together, this was not something familiar to Britain and wouldn't be until the 1930s, although it's fair to say roast dinners with roast potatoes didn't become commonplace until the 1950s.

The Book of Household Management *and Other Stories*

Roast Sirloin of Beef

Ingredients. – Beef, a little salt.

Mode. – As a joint cannot be well roasted without a good fire, see that it is well made up about ¾ hour before it is required, so that when the joint is put down, it is clear and bright. Choose a nice sirloin, the weight of which should not exceed 16lbs., as the outside would be too much done, whilst the inside would not be done enough. Spit it or hook it on to the jack firmly, dredge it slightly with flour, and place it near the fire at first …

Then draw it to a distance, and keep continually basting until the meat is done. Sprinkle a small quantity of salt over it, empty the dripping-pan of all the dripping, pour in some boiling water slightly salted, stir it about, and strain over the meat. Garnish with tufts of horseradish, and send horseradish sauce and Yorkshire pudding to table with it.

Time. – A sirloin of 10lbs., 2 1/2 hours; 14 to 16 lbs., about 4 or 4 ½ hours.

Average cost, 8 ½ d, per lb.

Sufficient, – A joint of 10lbs. for 8 or 9 persons

Seasonable at any time.[26]

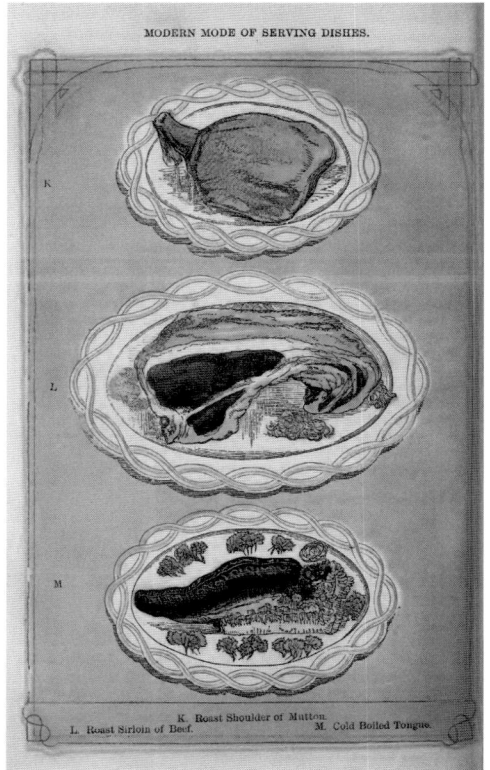

Two dishes you might expect to see in the *Book of Household Management*, but have been omitted, are cottage pie, or its lamb/mutton-based cousin, the shepherd's pie. Both were certainly established by then, although the

Illustration of Roast Beef from the *Book of Household Management.*

157

name cottage pie was more familiar than shepherd's, which was a Scottish term. Both cottage and shepherd's pie were hearty lunchtime meals like steak and kidney or sausages and baked potatoes and were sometimes just meat and mashed potato topped with pastry. Hunter's pie was another nineteenth-century favourite, a sort of layered Irish stew topped with mashed potato.

Beeton does, however, include an interesting recipe for potato pasty, which was actually the name of the tin vessel it was cooked in, as opposed to the dish itself.

The potato pasty pan was invented around 1815 and this slightly conical contraption had a lid pierced with holes which covered a tin plate of seasoned meat and gravy underneath. A layer of mashed potatoes was then piled on top of the perforated lid, the idea being that the flavoured steam from the meat below would infuse the potato topping.

Potato Pasty
Ingredients – 1 ½ lb. of rump-steak or mutton cutlets, pepper and salt to taste, ½ pint of weak broth or gravy, 1oz. of butter, mashed potatoes.

Mode – Place the meat, cut in small pieces, at the bottom of the pan; season it with pepper and salt, and add the gravy and butter broken into small pieces. Put on the perforated plate, with its valve-pipe screwed on, and fill up the whole space to the top of the tube with nicely mashed potatoes mixed with a little milk, and finish the surface of them in any ornamental manner. If carefully baked the potatoes will be covered with a delicate brown crust, retaining all the savoury steam rising from the meat. Send it to table as it comes from the oven, with a napkin folded round it.

Time – 40-60 minutes. Average cost 2s.

Sufficient for 4 or 5 persons. Seasonable at any time.[27]

Although dishes like shepherd's and cottage pie outdated the potato pasty, another historic recipe popular enough to stand the culinary test of time is Toad-in-the-Hole. Toad-in-the-Hole grew out of an eighteenth-century appetite for batter puddings and originally it was just a way of making leftover meat go a bit further on a plate, with the transition from meat scraps to sausages being a twentieth century one. It is also unlikely that any real toads were eaten as part of the meal, the name was probably more of a visual description of the final dish.

Here is Isabella's version of this classic recipe:

Toad-In-The-Hole

Ingredients. – 1 ½ lb. of rump steak, 1 sheep's kidney, pepper and salt to taste. For the batter, 3 eggs, 1 pint of milk, 4 tablespoons of flour, ½ saltspoonful of salt.

Mode. – Cut up the steak and kidney into convenient-sized pieces, and put them into a pie dish, with a good seasoning of salt and pepper; mix the flour with a small quantity of milk at first, to prevent its being lumpy; add the remainder and the 3 eggs, which should be well beaten; put in the salt, stir the batter for about 5 minutes, and pour it over the steak. Place it in a tolerably brisk oven immediately, and bake for 1 ½ hour.

Time. – 1 ½ hour. Average cost, 1s.9d.

Sufficient for 4 or 5 persons.

Seasonable at any time.

Note. – The remains of cold beef, rather underdone, may be substituted for the steak, and, when liked, the smallest possible quantity of minced onion or shallot may be added.[28]

The Bakewell Tart began its incarnation as a pudding, the earliest reference for which I can find being an 1833 recipe published in *Vegetable Cookery; With an Introduction, Recommending Abstinence from Animal Food and Intoxicating Liquors*. By the 1870s, it appears to have morphed into the Bakewell Tart. Beeton recommends Bakewell Pudding as an ideal plain family dessert recipe for December, and the *Derby Mercury* of 1841 noted that it was a 'far-famed' pudding.[29] The original dish was essentially a puff pastry shell, filled with jam and a sort of almond egg custard. Beeton's published version boasts a 'very rich' variant.

Bakewell Pudding

INGREDIENTS. – ¼ lb. of puff-paste, 5 eggs, 6oz. of sugar, ¼ lb of butter, 1oz. of almonds, jam.

Mode. – Cover a dish with thin paste, and put over this a layer of any kind of jam, ½ inch thick, put the yolks of 5 eggs into a basin with the white of 1, and beat these well; add the sifted sugar, the butter, which should be melted, and the almonds, which should be well pounded; beat all together until well mixed, then pour into the dish over the jam, and bake for an hour in a moderate oven.

Time. – 1 hour. *Average cost.* 1s, 6d.

Sufficient. For 4 or 5 persons. *Seasonable* at any time.[30]

There are literally hundreds of pottages, thick grain-based stews, and intestine-encased dishes in Britain's culinary past, so that it's futile to calculate precisely where today's Christmas pudding originated. Like many other late medieval puddings, it probably evolved from something like the ancient Roman wheat porridge called furmenty (frumenty/fermity/fromity). Furmenty was originally eaten during fasting days and in later years imported dried fruit was added and it became the number one dish to accompany group celebrations, gatherings, and Christmas festivities. By the 1700s, a 'Christmas plum porridge' was referenced widely in literature, the contents of which included a combination of meat, bread, dried fruit, sugar, wine, broth, cloves,

Recreation of Bakewell Pudding.
(© Emma Kay)

nutmeg, lemons, and so on, and this is when it came to resemble the plum pudding we are all now familiar with.

The word 'pudding' first appeared in the 1200s, and it probably heralded from the Anglo-Norman word *bodeyn/bodin*, translating as stuffed entrails, which evolved into the word 'pudding'. By the 1800s, a pudding meant anything boiled up in a bag – be it intestine or muslin. During a conversation about the origins of yuletide celebrations, a journalist once sarcastically remarked to me: 'Well, we all know that Charles Dickens invented Christmas.' But there is obviously something to be said about the way in which the Victorians revived this ancient custom and what better way than to put a plum pudding (plum being the once generic word for dried fruit) at the centre of it all, a pudding with a legacy steeped in customary celebrations, special events and social occasions.

Pick up almost any cookery book of the nineteenth century and you will find a recipe for plum pudding, Britain's national dish, and Isabella Beeton's iconic publication is no exception. There are over thirty references to plum pudding in the *Book of Household Management*, from numerous basic recipes to sauces to accompany it and menu recommendations. Plum pudding is as valued today as it was over 150 years ago.

Recreation of Plum Pudding Mix.
(© Emma Kay)

Christmas Plum Pudding (Very Good)

Ingredients. – 1 ½ lb. of raisins, ½ lb currants, ½ lb. of mixed peel, ¾ lb. of suet, 8 eggs, 1 wineglassful of brandy.

Mode. – Stone and cut the raisins in halves, but do not chop them; wash, pick, and dry the currants, and mince the suet finely; cut the candied peel into thin slices, and grate down the bread into fine crumbs.

When all these dry ingredients are prepared, mix them well together; then moisten the mixture with the eggs, which should be well beaten, and the brandy; stir well, that everything may be very thoroughly blended, and *press* the pudding into a buttered mould; tie it down tightly with a floured cloth. And boil for 5 or 6 hours. It may be boiled in a cloth without a mould, and will require the same time allowed for cooking. As Christmas puddings are usually made a few days before they are required for table when the pudding is taken out of the pot, hang it up immediately, and put a plate or saucer underneath to catch the water that may drain from it. The day it is to be eaten, plunge it into boiling water, and keep it boiling for at least 2 hours; then turn it out of the mould, and serve with brandy sauce. On Christmas-day a sprig of holly is usually placed in the middle of the pudding, and about a wineglassful of brandy poured round it, which at the moment of serving, is lighted, and the pudding thus brought to table encircled in flame.

Time. – 5 or 6 hours the first time of boiling; 2 hours the day it is to be served.

Average cost, 4s.

Sufficient for a quart mould for 7 or 8 persons.

Seasonable on the 25th of December, and on various festive occasions till March.

Note. – Five or six of these puddings should be made at one time, as they will keep good for many weeks, and in cases where unexpected guests arrive, will be found an acceptable, and, as it only requires warming through, a quickly-prepared dish. Moulds of every shape and size are manufactured for these.[31]

The recipes that got away

There are of course those recipes that inevitably didn't make it out of *The Englishwoman's Domestic Magazine* and into the *Book of Household Management*, like potato souffles, which did, however, find its way verbatim into Mrs Henry Lumpkin Wilson's *Tested Recipe Book* of 1895, which I'm fairly certain was soon after re-titled *The Atlanta Exposition Cookbook*. Interestingly this recipe is credited to a Mrs M. J. Speer, Atlanta.[32]

And yet it was published some forty years earlier in Isabella Beeton and Samuel Beeton's *Englishwoman's Domestic Magazine*, right down to the final sentence, which reads, 'If properly made they are extremely light, and are always liked.' This is interesting on so many levels as Mrs Lumpkin Wilson, wife of a renowned physician and Atlantan real estate executive, Henry Lumpkin Wilson, is understood to have collated all of these recipes as cherished Southern dishes passed down from mothers and grandmothers. Either the lady who contributed the recipe must have inherited it written exactly as it was from when it was published in *The Englishwoman's Domestic Magazine*, or she simply stole the recipe from the book to add to the collection. Whatever the reason for potato souffles turning up in Mrs Lumpkin Wilson's book on traditional Atlanta dishes, it shows just how far this humble recipe travelled.

> **Potato Souffles**
> Bake the potatoes till done, then cut a piece off large enough to allow of the inside being scooped out. Mix with a large piece of butter, cream, pepper, and salt. To every two potatoes one egg will be required. Mix the yolks well with the potatoes, whip the whites to a strong froth and lightly stir in; then fill the skins, put them into the oven, and bake a light brown. If properly made, they are extremely light, and are always liked.[33]

Another recipe that didn't measure up was Dutch Sweetbreads. The first reference I can find to Dutch Sweetbreads is in 1846 as part of a compendium of homeopathic recipes; there are a few variations, but it is generally veal, shaped like sweetbreads (animal pancreas or throat glands) breadcrumbed and fried. Here is the recipe as it appeared in a 1956 edition of *The Englishwoman's Domestic Magazine*.

Dutch Sweetbreads
Two pounds of veal; a quarter pound of suet chopped very fine; flour 'tops and bottoms', soaked in milk; a little lemon-peel grated fine; pepper, salt, and nutmeg to taste. Mix all well together with four eggs; make up in the shape of sweetbreads; rub over with egg and bread-crumbs, and fry of a light brown. Serve with gravy.[34]

Simple Sugar Cakes, with a recipe consisting of one pound of sugar and nine eggs, was another that failed to pass muster. Boasting a sell-by date of several months (undoubtedly due to all that sugar), it would be interesting to determine how Isabella ultimately chose which recipes to add to her seminal volume.

Sugar Cakes
One pound of flour, one pound of loaf-sugar, nine eggs, a quarter of a pound of butter, a few drops of any essence you like. Mix altogether well with a spoon. Drop it on your tins, not a very hot oven. A quarter of this receipt makes a nice dishful; but they will keep for months in a dry place.[35]

The sugar cake recipe was an established one in the nineteenth century, with many superior versions including Eliza Acton's, which appeared in her *Modern Cookery for Private Families*, encouraging the addition of spices, currants, and the consistency of a rolled paste.[36] Perhaps the simplicity of *The Englishwoman's Domestic Magazine* recipe was not dynamic enough to find a place in Isabella's collective culinary manual.

The Italian cheese recipe reproduced in Volume 5 of *The Englishwoman's Domestic Magazine* is, I assume, a basic

Recreation of Sugar Cakes. (© Emma Kay)

mascarpone. While the *Book of Household Management* contains a section devoted to cheese, there aren't that many actual cheese recipes, with one for Stilton, which Beeton refers to as 'British Parmesan', dominating this category. English Parmesan, it seems, was in fact a term used to describe Stilton cheese throughout the eighteenth and nineteenth centuries, a light-hearted approach comparing the popularity of parmesan in Italy with that of Stilton in England. Perhaps the fact that Beeton's cheese section places Stilton at the heart of it suggests she was looking to showcase British cheese and this is why the Italian cheese recipe didn't recommend itself to the *Book of Household Management*. I've included it here as it's a lovely straightforward recipe.

Italian Cheese
To a pint of scalded cream, whipped very smooth, add the juice of three lemons, and the rind of two – sugar to taste; let it stand for half an hour, then whip till it is very thick, tie it in a thin cloth, or a tin with holes in it; let it drain till next day, then turn out.[37]

Another simple dish that clearly wasn't suited to the household manual was parsnip pudding, which I must admit doesn't sound hugely appetising, unless you have a special fondness for this root vegetable.

Parsnip Pudding
Parsnip pudding is made by boiling two parsnips, draining the water from them, mashing them, and adding grated bread, the yolks of two eggs, sugar and spice to the taste, and a little cream; the whole, when mixed, is poured into a light puff paste and baked.[38]

Drinks

In comparison with Isabella Beeton, there are very few references to drinks in the work of Agnes Marshall, aside from a couple including currant water and a frozen Roman punch, which Marshall most insistently stresses had replaced the standard punch drink by the 1880s. The frozen Roman punch recipe variation included in her *Book of Ices* does indeed appear to have become very popular by the latter part of the nineteenth century. In fact, the demise of punch, emphasised by Agnes, is echoed in *Mrs Beeton's Book of Household Management* some twenty or so years earlier, with the author observing:

> Punch is a beverage made of various spirituous liquors or wine, hot water, the acid juice of fruits, and sugar. It is considered to be very intoxicating punch, which was almost universally drunk among the middle classes about fifty or sixty years ago, has almost disappeared from our domestic tables, being superseded by wine. There are many different varieties of punch.

Isabella cites the North American 'mint julep' as the 'most inviting' summer punch and quotes a recipe by the English Victorian author and Royal Navy Officer Captain Frederick Marryat:

> Put into a tumbler about a dozen sprigs of the tender shoots of mint; upon them put a spoonful of white sugar, and equal proportions of peach and common brandy, so as to fill up one third, or, perhaps, a little less; then take rasped or pounded ice, and fill up the tumbler. Epicures rub the lips of the tumbler with a piece of fresh pineapple; and the tumbler itself is very often encrusted outside with stalactites of ice. As the ice melts, you drink.[39]

Another drink which has disappeared from our tables is Negus, once a highly fashionable hot and spiced wine which is a requested refreshment of the eponymous heroine of Charlotte Bronte's novel *Jane Eyre*, and in Jane Austen's *Mansfield Park*, it is served at a ball alongside soup.[40] Negus is also mentioned throughout many of the works of Charles Dicken, most notably in *The Pickwick Papers*, as a strong, intoxicating drink,[41] and as an accompaniment to cake, roast meats, and mince pies at Fezziwig's Christmas party in *A Christmas Carol*.[42] Negus is also cited as the only thing to distract a man away from a beautiful woman in William Makepeace Thackeray's 1840s bestseller, *Vanity Fair*.[43]

Interestingly, Mrs Beeton describes the drink as one which was most frequently drunk at children's parties, which rather contradicts its heady place in Regency and Victorian literature, unless the children's parties she frequented were rather racier than expected.

To Make Negus
Ingredients. – To every pint of port wine allow 1 quart of boiling water, ¼ lb. of sugar, 1 lemon, grated nutmeg to taste. Mode. – Put the wine into a jug, rub some lumps of sugar (equal to ¼ lb) on the lemon-rind until all the yellow part of the skin is absorbed, then squeeze the juice, and strain it. Add the sugar and lemon-juice to the port wine, with the grated nutmeg; pour over it the boiling water, cover the jug, and, when the beverage has cooled a little, it will be fit for use.

Negus may also be made of sherry, or any other sweet white wine, but is more usually made of port than of any other beverage.[44]

Sufficient. – allow 1 pint of wine, with the other ingredients in proportion, for a party of 9 or 10 children.

In her section on 'Invalid Cooking', Isabella includes a recipe for Egg Wine. This is reminiscent of the medieval caudles and possets that were combinations of eggs and milk, or milk and wine, which unless you count the lasting popularity of eggnog have all but disappeared in the twenty-first century. Such drinks were considered restorative and administered to new mothers, people who were ill, and even as an offering to the land in the Highlands of Scotland.[45]

Nowadays you're more likely to find people adding eggs to drinks to aid a hangover, so perhaps some of those theories about restoring strength have endured.

Egg Wine
INGREDIENTS. – 1 egg, 1 tablespoonful and ½ glass of cold water, 1 glass of sherry, sugar, and grated nutmeg to taste.

Mode. – Beat the egg, mixing with it a tablespoonful of cold water; make the wine-and-water hot, but not boiling; pour it on the egg, stirring all the time. Add sufficient lump sugar to sweeten the mixture, and a little grated nutmeg; put all into a very clean saucepan, set it on a gentle fire, and stir the contents one way until they thicken, *but do not allow them to boil.* Serve in a glass with sippets of toasted bread or plain, crisp biscuits. When the egg is not warmed, the mixture will be found easier of digestion, but it is not so pleasant drink.[46]

The rights to the Beeton cookery books were sold to First National Finance in 1972 for £250,000 as part of a takeover bid for publishers Ward Lock, who incidentally were also the owners of Agnes B. Marshall's publishing rights.

Chapter 5

Day-to-Day Lives, Pinner and Peers

Both Agnes and Isabella were running food-related enterprises in nineteenth-century London, although it's fair to say Agnes's was certainly the more challenging business.

By the time Isabella's culinary work came to fruition, London was the hub of the European urban market. Smithfield meat market was still being built in Isabella's lifetime. It would be Agnes who would benefit from the supplies of fresh cuts from this butchers' palace, although both would have enjoyed the delights of Covent Garden's covered fruit and vegetable market, just a twenty-minute walk from Marshall's School of Cookery.

Grocery stores have been on the streets of England since the 1600s. They sold a combination of staple commodities and luxury imported goods, such as coffee, chocolate, tea, sugar, and spices. The Company of Grossers, which eventually morphed into Grocers, was founded in London as early as 1373; the term grocer was generally used for someone who sold items in bulk (gross). These were shops that catered to both the wealthy and the poor in different ways. While the privileged benefitted from products on credit, the labouring classes were served out of a window, typically on a cash purchase basis. Most of the major supermarkets we are familiar with today started out as grocery stores. Lancashire's famous chain of food stores, Booths, was one of the first, established in 1847, followed by Sainsbury's in 1869, although the single horse van delivering goods around Pinner from the Sainsbury's store in Greenhill would not become a regular feature until the start of the twentieth century.

Again, it would be Agnes and her generation who gained the advantage of larger, more convenient stores such as this. Isabella would have made do with the street markets and general grocers. Whether she visited these herself is debatable. She certainly talks in generic terms about the London marketplace as a whole, listing the sources of products in her *Book of Household Management* like fish coming from the east coast, as well as the Thames, specifically citing the best plaice to be found in Hastings and Folkestone, bream from Cornwall, and sprats from Suffolk, Essex, and Kent. This was an age of seasonal produce. Overseas food imports were largely luxury items. Britain yielded its own rich and bountiful sources of meat, fish, dairy, vegetables, and grains. Of course, most provisions were delivered to your door if you had the money.

It's interesting to see as a society how we have now gone full circle with this method of retail exchange, with most farm shops, butchers, and supermarkets providing a doorstep delivery service today. This type of pre-order resource must have required a great deal of organisation and planning, particularly if you were testing recipes. Not only would you need to make decisions regarding your ingredients, but you also had to plan your own weekly meals in advance too. Of course, housekeepers, if you were privileged enough to have one, could be tasked with this job, but it would still need to be communicated by the lady of the house.

Isabella certainly didn't have a housekeeper, but we know Agnes did. I wonder if this made life easier or harder in terms of ensuring you had everything to hand before cooking. What about all those last-minute missing items? I have visions of Isabella scrawling notes with 'pick up eggs and extra flour on way home', before entrusting a small boy with a shiny coin and sending him off to the city to deliver it with haste to Samuel. Again, Agnes had the luxury of swift underground rail travel or even the motor car if she needed to access London; Isabella may have had access to a cart, or there was the horse-drawn omnibus. By the 1850s, the London General Omnibus Company was heralded as the largest bus company in the world.[2] There was also the pleasure boat on the canal which escorted day trippers between Pinner and London and of course Pinner mainline overground station (now known as Hatch End) into London, which opened in 1844. I think the line may always have linked directly to Euston Square. Today this service takes around an hour each way. Isabella and Samuel's house has been described as isolated within the village, while Agnes and Alfred lived just a short distance from the underground station.[3]

This may well have been claustrophobic for Isabella, cut off from society, immersed in her kitchen trialling and rejecting recipes for her magnum opus, suffering the mortifying cruelties of miscarriage and infant death alone, with a frequently absent father and a family rapidly becoming estranged. Perhaps this is one of the reasons why the couple chose to move back into London in 1863 and then on to Greenhithe, Kent, unaware that Isabella would die trying to create that family, to bring their young children up in more salubrious surroundings.

So, what could you expect to find in Pinner when both ladies lived there? A coach ran regularly from the Queens Head into London during both their lifetimes. Did either of them take advantage of it? If they did, it would be more likely to have been Isabella. What was once identified as the Equestrian Villa in Pinner High Street became a fashionable coffee tavern and chocolate house, Ye Cocoa Tree, popular with local cyclists passing by when Agnes lived locally. Along this same street stood a butcher's shop which is perhaps where both Isabella and Agnes had their meat delivered from; alternatively, Agnes may have frequented the later established George Hedges's butcher's shop in Bridge Street and the confectioner's run by his daughter next door.

Would Samuel or Alfred have supped a half pint in the Queens Head, which remains today as an example of beautiful sixteenth-century ale house architecture? Although heavy drinking women of nineteenth-century working-class London were an acceptable sight in the inns and taverns, middle-class women certainly would not have been, unless they were awaiting a carriage, of course. Public drinking was even more of a taboo for women in rural areas and many public houses had segregated bars or even just a hatch with which to serve women a jug of ale to take home. That's not to say women from wealthier classes didn't drink. In fact, women probably consumed more alcohol through their belief in daily medicated wines than anything else. Neither Agnes nor Isabella lived to see the act removing sexual discrimination in 1919, just fourteen years after Agnes died. Women were no longer denied involvement in any public function or duty after this legislation. It would be interesting to see how they both responded to this in their private and work lives. Their generation was really the last of the out and out struggle for women, although some would say it's still as relevant today, of course.

There was even a windmill on Pinner Hill Road, which both families would have enjoyed. Did Isabella and Agnes acquire their grain and flour from here and make bread from its freshly ground resources?[4]

The annual Pinner Fair once sold livestock and produce aplenty, which morphed into a purely recreational fairground as the industrial revolution progressed. Isabella herself may have attended. Harrow weekly market, which once served the whole area, had disappeared by the 1500s, with Pinner relying on London to accommodate the majority of its comestible needs.

Pinner Village, 1907.

Although Isabella and Samuel moved to Kent not long after the success of the *Book of Household Management*, she had written it while living in Pinner and presumably this is where she tried and tested most of the recipes. Isabella's kitchen would not have had electricity, perhaps not even gas, but we do know that she had the help of at least one general house servant and a nursemaid, employed to look after Samuel Orchart, whose life would turn out to be a very short one.

Childcare was not an issue for either Agnes or Isabella. Lucky them, many women would not have had that support, particularly working-class labouring women who toiled in the factories, back-street sweat shops, or market stalls. The term 'baby farming', referred to earlier, defined many aspects of the trade, from women offering to 'adopt' children into their homes for a fee, to the darker side of murder and discreet burial. The reality is that many children of the Victorian age were at best hugely neglected, at worst just disposed of by any means. Baby farming was, however, beginning to become recognised by the 1860s and public campaigns, most notably led by the *British Medical Journal*, were set in motion to expose these crimes and eradicate the horrors of their actions.

Having staff who could assist Isabella and Agnes, the latter benefitting from employees at both home and in the workplace, removed many of the daily stresses that remained relentless for working-class women, stresses which we can only imagine must have forced them to make some terrible decisions. Without work you had no shelter or food, but having children meant you were unable to work. Remember these were the days before the Welfare State. It's no wonder many women tried to set themselves up with a skill like sewing, weaving, or taking in laundry which could be done at home. By the time of the industrial revolution however, many of these tasks could be achieved more labour intensively in the factories. There were also those who went to work as domestic staff for women like Isabella and Agnes and you certainly couldn't take your children into these environments.

Unlike the slightly more advanced kitchen that Agnes would have utilised at home, although we can't know for sure, Isabella probably had a kitchen in which the central feature was a long wooden table, which served as the main preparation area, a place to sit and rest and of course taste test, surrounded by moveable, heavy wooden storage furniture, with mostly open shelves, an open-hearth stove, and a sink. Isabella's stove may well have been one of the new enclosed varieties, which was beginning to revolutionise the way people cooked. You might expect to still spend about six hours or more a day in the kitchen prepping and cooking, with even further hours taken up with cleaning. Isabella didn't have a cook, but we know she had some help. There would perhaps still have been a well for water, which would not have been sanitary. As to whether the Beetons had gas, this is, as previously suggested, contentious. Isabella does talk about gas coking as no longer being a novelty and a labour-saving grace in her *Book of Household Management* but she is also critical of it, like the consequences of forgetting to turn the gas supply off and the need to be fully trained in the ways of using it to cook effectively. This was a common misconception in the early days of gas consumption. We are reminded that her era was still largely about cooking on spits on an open fire, using smoke jacks (several spits turning at the same time), bottle-jacks to hang meat to roast over the hearth and gridirons (a sort of portable grill).

Agnes talks about using a 'grill iron', which may have been more of a cast-iron plate, as opposed to the more archaic grid. Salamanders, a sort of

Above left: Victorian roasting jack, from the collection of Emma Kay. (© Emma Kay)

Above right: Victorian grid iron, from the collection of Emma Kay. (© Emma Kay)

long-handled iron spoon, heated to toast or brown the surfaces of food was used into and beyond the 1890s, but while Isabella was finely chopping her meat while wielding a large sharp knife, Agnes had moved onto the new labour-saving mincing machines. The market was flooded with grinders, choppers, and even slicers of all kinds by the latter part of the nineteenth century.

Both ladies would have benefitted from chafing dishes to keep food warm at the table. They would have cooked with sauté pans, weighed ingredients on modern weighing machines, as opposed to old balance scales, used steamers, fish kettles, a variety of moulds in differing shapes and sizes and drained food in colanders, cooked in tinned copper pans and milled chocolate – a practice which was most associated with the Georgian era but remained popular well into the twentieth century.

Isabella undoubtedly owned a basic lead-lined ice chest or box to keep perishables slightly colder than warm; she wouldn't have witnessed the advancements Agnes made with her ice cave and ice freezer. Sugar beet had replaced cane sugar by the 1880s and powdered down sugar, called 'castor sugar', was more readily available. In fact, this was being advertised in Isabella's lifetime, but she makes no mention of it in her *Book of Household*

Above left: Early twentieth-century meat grinder, from the collection of Emma Kay. (© Emma Kay)

Above right: Bean slicer, from the collection of Emma Kay. (© Emma Kay)

Victorian objects and Georgian chocolate mill, from the collection of Emma Kay. (© Emma Kay)

Management. Agnes, however, refers to it regularly within her *Larger Cookery Book*. As someone who has recreated old recipes using traditional methods, I can vouch for the fact that pounding down sugar from its loaf form in a pestle and mortar is a painstaking labour of love.

Another unfamiliar item to Isabella would have been the rotary-style handheld mixer. While early inventions circulated in the 1860s, they weren't popularised until around the time of Agnes's death. Agnes is likely to have used a potato ricer too, a utensil Isabella would only have dreamed of, with its perforated holes, similar to a garlic press, squeezing potatoes into manageable strands. In fact, if Agnes had lived just a little longer, she would have marvelled at the invention of the Aga cooker, the dawn of electric cooking, the emergence of pressure cookers, aluminium cookware, and even one of the first electric marmalade cutters, advertised as early as 1905.[5]

Middle-class kitchens by the late nineteenth century were vastly improved and new houses being built in 1900 would all most certainly have had a purpose-built kitchen, as opposed to just a space with a hearth. Agnes, I'm certain, would have adapted both her kitchens at home and at Marshall's to incorporate many of these new additions.

Gas and coal were the main sources of energy and to encourage fuel efficiency, grates and adjustable canopies to control air flow were integral to all fireplaces. Ranges were enclosed with sliding panels to alternate between fireplace and stove. Slowly the dual-purpose stove became a single unit just for cooking. Despite domestic water supply systems being available as early as the 1600s, believe it or not, improvements and greater access to nationalised filtered mains water supplies meant no more treks to the well and fewer ways to contract a disease. The kitchen began to be a very practical place, with proper cabinets designed to store a range of new and improved kitchen utensils and work surfaces to chop and prepare food. By the first decade of the twentieth century, every fashionable kitchen of the wealthy in Ireland would have a Hoosier cabinet. This was an American import combining table and storage, boasting space for 400 items. It would take another ten years or so before this then became a staple of the English kitchen too.

The extent to which we rely on gadgets and convenience products in the modern age would have been mind-blowing to Isabella and Agnes. If their time had been this time, would both ladies have achieved something even greater, and was their success just a product of the age? They did, after all, have the support of their wealthy, influential spouses, together with the wherewithal to create something new and dynamic in an industrial utopian world. They made sacrifices, though, and must have experienced the limitations of their own sex many times over, at a point in history when women fought fiercely for enfranchisement.

There is also something quite unsettling about the process of food writing and the food industry generally in Victorian London. The disparity between not having access to even any form of basic nourishment and training women to cook elaborate dishes for wealthy households who had an abundance is abhorrent if you stop and think about it.

Isabella Beeton's beloved Paris, which she and Samuel frequented to extol its fashionable virtues within the pages of their magazines, was still in many ways recovering from the atrocities of the revolution. Charles Dickens illustrates the hardships of eighteenth-century Paris which he interwove symbolically with the streets of nineteenth-century London:

> … the children had ancient faces and grave voices; and upon them, and upon the grown faces and ploughed into every furrow of age and coming up afresh, was the sign, Hunger. It was prevalent everywhere. Hunger was pushed out of the tall houses, in the wretched clothing that hung upon poles and lines; Hunger was patched into them with straw and rag and wood and paper; Hunger was repeated in every fragment of the small modicum of firewood that the man sawed off;

Hunger stared down from the smokeless chimneys, and stared up from the filthy street that had no offal, among its refuse, of anything to eat. Hunger was the inscription on the baker's shelves, written in every small loaf of his scanty stock of bad bread; at the sausage shop, in every dead-dog preparation that was offered for sale. Hunger rattled its dry bones among the roasting chestnuts in the turned cylinder; Hunger was shred into atomies in every farthing porringer of husky chips, fried with some reluctant drops of oil.[6]

There's no argument for suggesting that food writers and food businesses should have been more sensitive and not forged ahead with their achievements, but there is perhaps an argument for proposing that both Agnes and Isabella could have done more to impart their knowledge for the benefit of society generally. Particularly Agnes, whose school did little to train those who most needed it, even charging their students for leftover ingredients, which could have fed the poor. In comparison, Victorian celebrity chef Alexis Soyer was so concerned with the state of food poverty that in 1855 he wrote the practical manual, *A Shilling Cookery for the People*, aimed at educating those people in society who were ignorant of the economies of cooking. Soyer worked for the wealthy clientele of London's famous Reform Club, but he also worked as a government adviser, establishing large-scale soup kitchens across Ireland to assist with famine relief, and mobilised field and military hospital kitchens in the Crimea. Soyer also made door-to-door visits, going into the homes of everyday folk to research and give counsel.

In his letters, he mentions attending several colliers' cottages; during one of these visits, Soyer observed a piece of meat having been recently roasted and left in a pan. The meat was overcooked and dried out and being left next to the fire, it continued to disintegrate. It turned out that the meat itself wasn't central to the family's requirements. They were simply draining the excess fat to make puddings. Soyer calculated that the joint of meat would have weighed in the region of five pounds prior to cooking, which reduced to three after. The family paid around 40 pence for the uncooked meat, when a piece of fat for their purposes cost just 5 pence.[7]

A similar attempt was made by former chef to Queen Victoria, Charles Elme Francatelli, whose *A Plain Cookery Book for the Working Classes* of

1852 has a chatty, unpretentious, and warm approach, reaching out to those who had no time, knowledge of or inclination to cook: 'To those of my readers who, from sickness or other hindrance, have not money in store, I would say, strive to lay by a little of your weekly wages to purchase these things, that your families may be well fed, and your homes made comfortable.'[8]

Agnes and Isabella were so busy advising the middle classes and all the new wealth that was garnered from this, they neglected the very people who needed them most. We do know that Isabella helped out in local soup kitchens and it's likely that Agnes may have had some sort of philanthropic duty, it's just not been recorded.

There were many other culinary writers and food champions of the Victorian era. Eliza Acton died a few years after Agnes was born, but she would have been familiar with her writing, of course. Eliza was one of the first cookery writers to include timings, weights, and measures and Isabella Beeton is often accused of replicating her style and plagiarising her work, although she does mention her by name once in the *Book of Household Management*.

Agnes only referenced renowned French male chefs.

May Byron straddled both the nineteenth and twentieth centuries. She wrote an excellent book of puddings and a helpful guide to rationing among others, which neither Agnes nor Isabella got the chance to read. Another lesser-known cookery writer of the Victorian age was Arthur Gay Payne. He was also a journalist and editor of numerous periodicals, including sporting magazines, so it's likely he moved in the same circles as Samuel Beeton, although this would have been towards the very end of Samuel's career. Payne was also entwined with aspects of the Victorian blockbuster publication company, Cassell's. His *Cassell's Shilling Cookery* book of 1888 strongly echoes Isabella's work and is pitched at a middle-class readership. It is very reminiscent of *Mrs Beeton's Dictionary of Every-Day Cookery*, the book she was writing just before her death.

Lesser-known Victorian cookery writers who nonetheless made an impression during their lifetime include Scottish-born Margaret Pearson, who trained at the National Training School in London and worked for a time at the Dundee School of Cookery in addition to selling some 16,000 copies of her *Cookery Recipes for the People* in 1888. She went on to forge a significant career in Australia as a cookery teacher and demonstrator. Dubbed the 'Scottish Mrs Beeton' (I do wish journalists wouldn't do that), Christina Jane Johnstone, AKA Margaret Dods, wrote the widely critically acclaimed *Cook and Housewife's Manual* in 1862. Then there were the hugely influential French chefs like Escoffier, Gouffe, and Americanised restaurateur and author Charles Ranhofer. Charles Herman Senn, mentioned previously as an editor of a later edition of the *Book of Household Management*, was, you guessed it, christened the 'British Soyer' by the press, cut his culinary teeth in Switzerland before embarking on a brilliant career in London as a chef, secretary of the London Annual Cookery and Food Exhibitions for the illustrious Universal Cookery and Food Association, government advisor on naval cookery, and author of numerous culinary texts.[9]

One of Agnes's rivals at the time, although her philosophies and objectives were very different, was Christian Edington Guthrie Wright and her partner Louisa Stevenson, who founded the Edinburgh School of Cookery and Domestic Economy. In contrast to Agnes, the Edinburgh school, which was founded in 1875, was dedicated to both enhancing the education of women and improving the diets of the working classes. Guthrie Wright lectured and trained many of the students herself; like Agnes she toured, unlike Agnes she helped develop other similar institutions and established a school in Manchester as well as building relationships to progress this cause with like-mended trainers, including Edith Nicolls of London's own National Training School and Fanny Calder of Liverpool School of Cookery, which was one of the first; like Guthrie Wright's Edinburgh enterprise, to follow in the footsteps of the original London school, opening in 1875, and Grace Paterson, who ran the Glasgow School of Cookery, also started in 1875.

Christian compiled the very influential *School Cookery Book* which focused on basic, economic cooking. This no-nonsense guide opens with a preface explaining that the use of simple language, minimal ingredients, and unadorned directions are necessary for a book written for the purposes of elementary school cookery classes. There's no French language, no symphony of complimentary dishes, just practical recipes like potato soup, fish pudding, brain cakes, and my particular favourite, which appears in numerous cookery books throughout the late Victorian and early twentieth century, Poor Man's Goose, the variations of which always consist of alternate layers of different components like offal, bacon, fruit, or herbs. I'm not sure how this compares to goose, but maybe the richness of the dish using cheap cuts made it taste like a luxury meal.

Poor Man's Goose
Required: A sheep's liver and heart; ½ lb. fat bacon; about 1 teaspoonful powdered sage; 2 onions (previously boiled); 1oz flour; ½ oz. dripping; 1 gill cold water; ¼ teaspoonful salt; ¼ teaspoonful pepper.

Wash and dry the liver and heart thoroughly; cut them into thin slices; dip each slice into the flour. Chop the onions; cut the bacon into thin slices and remove the rind. Place a layer of heart and liver in the bottom of a greased pie dish; sprinkle over it a little of the chopped onion, sage, pepper and salt; place a layer of bacon; repeat this till the materials (except the dripping) are all in the dish. Add the cold water. Cover the dish with a greased paper; bake in a moderate oven for about an hour.[10]

The power of these institutions and the stories of the women behind them are awe inspiring. They led to the establishment of university colleges and consortiums like the Northern Union of Training Schools of Cookery. They were entrenched in the suffrage movement and provided the foundations for all future learning within the arena of Domestic Science. It's difficult to compare them with the work of Agnes and Alfred Marshall, as they had completely different objectives, but it's also important to recognise the difference between a money-making training enterprise and a benevolent one in Victorian Britain. It's possible to predict how the two could have mutually benefitted each other. I wonder if the likes of Guthrie Wright, Edith Nicolls, Grace Paterson, or Fanny Calder ever reached out to Agnes, or vice versa, they were each other's peers after all, breaking new ground in the birth of cookery instruction albeit in very different institutions which were attached to official governing bodies. In particular, Edith was living and working in the same sector as Agnes at the same time in London. Surely there must have been some sort of shared dialogue between the two. Edith also became an author of note in her own right, taking the pen name Mrs Charles Clarke, like so many did when they married. I also wonder if Isabella's book provided inspiration for later Victorian instructors of Domestic Science, with its fresh, pragmatic approach to cooking and housekeeping.

It's worth mentioning that the United States were also pioneers of training, with the majority of their university colleges offering provision to

Photograph of Mrs Charles Clarke. (Taken from *The Lady's Realm*, 1902)

instruct female students in housekeeping and cookery in makeshift model homes on site. The renowned Boston Cooking School, founded in 1879 and headed up by the equally celebrated American cook and author of the *Boston Cooking-School Cook Book*, Fannie Merrit Farmer, is just one example. Encarnacion Pinedo, a Spanish settler in the US, published her 800-odd Spanish and Mexican recipe compilation *El Cocinero Espanol* in 1898, while other American culinary writers and cooks like Mary Randolph, former slave Abbey Fisher, Eliza Leslie, who launched her own periodical as early as 1843, and pastry shop and cookery school owner of the early 1800s, Elizabeth Goodfellow, exemplify just a few.[11]

Agnes and Isabella were by no means the only ones. If you search the archives there are tens, if not hundreds of women who were working in the progressive food industry at this time, not just in Britain, but globally, labouring and creating in their own radical spaces. This book just covers two of those narratives. I encourage you to go and seek others out, learn both about and from their inspirational and forgotten journeys.

Notes

Introduction

1. De Ridder, J., Van Remoortel, M., 'Not "Simply Mrs. Warren": Eliza Warren Francis (1810–1900) and the "Ladies" Treasury', *Victorian Periodicals Review*, vol. 44, no. 4 (The John Hopkins University Press, 2011).

Chapter 1: Agnes Bertha Marshall

1. *The Table*, June 1886.
2. British Newspaper Archive, *The Uxbridge & W. Drayton Gazette* (5 August 1905).
3. British Newspaper Archive, *Daily Telegraph & Courier* (London) (1 September 1911).
4. British Newspaper Archive, *Pall Mall Gazette* (14 October 1886).
5. British Newspaper Archive, *Cardiff Times* (12 February 1887).
6. British Newspaper Archive, *Brighton Gazette* (5 May 1853).
7. British Newspaper Archive, *Ludlow Advertiser* (27 October 1900).
8. British Newspaper Archive, *Ludlow Advertiser* (7 May 1904).
9. British Newspaper Archive, *Kensington Post* (10 March 1961).
10. 1939 England & Wales Registrar, Ethel Newman, www.ancestry.co.uk/discoveryui-content/view/6155066:61596?tid=174613196&pid=182268007937&queryId=902d5ed6e366c5f6640fcf08f63d6e33&_phsrc=jzI1058&_phstart=successSource (accessed 4 January 2021).
11. National probate calendar 1858–1995, Ethel Newman, www.ancestry.co.uk/discoveryui-content/view/15658229:1904?tid=174613196&pid=182268007937&queryId=ab1977524c53fb5346000990d0d807be&_phsrc=jzI1070&_phstart=successSource (accessed 4 January 2021).

12. British Newspaper Archive, *The Edinburgh Gazette* (22 April 1924).
13. England & Wales, National Probate Calendar (Index of Wills and Administrations), 1858–1995 for Agnes Alfreda Marshall, 1935, ancestry.co.uk (accessed 4 January 2021).
14. 1891 English Census for Ethel Marshall, www.ancestry.co.uk/imageviewer/collections/6598/images/SSXRG12_803_805-0161?pId=12404154 (accessed 4 January 2021).
15. British Newspaper Archive, *The Daily Telegraph* (27 February 1904).
16. British Newspaper Archive, *Harrow Observer* (19 June 1908).
17. British Newspaper Archive, *Uxbridge & West Drayton Gazette* (1 October 1904).
18. British Newspaper Archive, *West London Observer* (6 September 1935).
19. British Newspaper Archive, *London Evening Standard* (3 December 1913).
20. British Newspaper Archive, *Lloyd's Weekly Newspaper* (14 February 1897).
21. Proceedings of the Central Criminal Court, 8th February 1897, Old Bailey online, www.oldbaileyonline.org/images.jsp?doc=189702080010 (accessed 4 September 2021).
22. British Newspaper Archive, *Harrow Observer* (8 July 1910).
23. Pinner Local History Society, www.pinnerlhs.org.uk/search (accessed 12 September 2021).
24. British Newspaper Archive, *The Cheltenham Examiner* (2 August 1905).
25. British Newspaper Archive, *Harrow Observer* (17 July 1914).
26. British Newspaper Archive, *Aldershot Military Gazette* (12 April 1879).
27. Talbot, V. A., *What to Do with Our Girls; or, Employments for Women* (Houlston & Sons, London, 1884).
28. *The Lancet* (1885), 34.
29. Google Patents, https://patents.google.com/patent/GB189423426A/en?assignee=Alfred+William+Marshall&oq=Alfred+William+Marshall (accessed 2 August 2021).
30. Theodore, F. G., *The Encyclopædia of Practical Cookery: A Complete Dictionary of All Pertaining to the Art of Cookery and Table Service* (Upcott Gill, London, 1892).

Notes

31. *Harrow Observer* (5 Oct 1906).
32. 1891 English Census for Gertrude Walsh, www.ancestry.co.uk/imageviewer/collections/6598/images/LNDRG12_469_472-0657?pId=8571816 (accessed 4 January 2021).
33. *Harrow Observer* (23 July 1897).
34. *Harrow Observer* (23 February 1917).
35. England & Wales, National Probate Calendar (Index of Wills and Administrations)1858–1995, for Alfred William Marshall, www.ancestry.co.uk/imageviewer/collections/1904/images/31874_223137-00175?pId=6021031 (accessed 5 October 2021).
36. *The Times*, St Stephen's Review (2 May 1887).
37. Kay, Emma, *Dining with the Georgians* (Amberley Publishing, Stroud, 2014), 132–133.
38. *Morning Post* (14 November 1883).
39. *Pall Mall Gazette* (14 October 1886).
40. *Cheltenham Examiner* (27 October 1886).
41. *The Queen* (13 April 1895).
42. *The Queen* (17 February 1900).
43. *Truth*, Vol. 33: January–June (London, 1893), 372.
44. *The Times* (11 May 1895).
45. *The Times* (2 July 1898).
46. *The Queen*, Saturday (23 June 1900).
47. *The Queen*, Saturday (13 June 1903).
48. *The Queen*, Saturday (4 July 1903).
49. *The Queen*, Saturday (30 March 1895).
50. Ibid.
51. Ibid.
52. Ibid.
53. Ibid.
54. *Edinburgh Evening News* (28 April 1925).
55. *The Times* (28 February 1940).
56. Jerome K. Jerome. (ed.), *To-Day: A Weekly Magazine-Journal*, Vol. 7 (Howard House, London, 1895), 42.
57. *The Queen* (13 April 1895).
58. *Morning Post* (30 January 1893).
59. *The United Opinion* (28 September 1888).
60. *Pall Mall Gazette* (14 October 1886).

61. Kay, Emma, *Cooking Up History: Chefs of the Past* (Prospect Books, London, 2017).
62. *Birmingham Daily Post* (10 August 1887).
63. *The Gas World*, Vol. 18 (John Allan, London, 1893), 79.
64. *Newcastle Daily Chronicle* (22 September 1892).
65. *Hull Daily Mail* (10 January 1893).
66. *Truth* (15 September 1892).
67. *Truth* (17 August 1905).
68. Ibid.
69. *The Dundee Advertiser* (28 September 1892).
70. *The Coffee Public-House News* (1885).
71. *Cardiff Times* (12 February 1887).

Chapter 2: The Recipes of Agnes Bertha Marshall

1. Marshall, A., *Mrs A. B. Marshall's Cookery Book* (Simpkin, Marshall, Hamilton, Kent & Co. Ltd, London, 1890).
2. Geddes, Kevin, *Keep Calm and Fanny On! The Many Careers of Fanny Craddock* (Fantom Publishing, Croydon, 2019), 67–69.
3. Craddock, F., *The Sherlock Holmes Cookbook* (W. H. Allen, London, 1976), 158–159.
4. Marshall, A., *Mrs A. B. Marshall's Cookery Book* (Simpkin, Marshall, Hamilton, Kent & Co. Ltd, London, 1890).
5. Ibid., 5.
6. *Larousse Gastronomique* (Paul Hamlyn Ltd, London, 1961).
7. Gouffe, Jules, *The Royal Cookery Book* (Sampson Low, Son, and Marston, 1869, London), 118.
8. Marshall, A., *Mrs A. B. Marshall's Cookery Book* (Simpkin, Marshall, Hamilton, Kent & Co. Ltd, London, 1890), 219.
9. Acton, E., *Modern Cookery in All Its Branches* (Lea and Blanchard, Philadelphia and London, 1845), 256.
10. Beeton, I., *The Book of Household Management* (S. O. Beeton, London, 1861), 482.
11. British Newspaper Archive, *The Cheltenham Examiner* (2 August 1905).
12. British Newspaper Archive, *The Yorkshire Post* (1 November 1886).

13. Marshall, A., *Mrs A. B. Marshall's Cookery Book* (Simpkin, Marshall, Hamilton, Kent & Co. Ltd, London, 1890), 279.
14. British Newspaper Archive, *Truth* (13 July 1893).
15. British Newspaper Archive, *Cheltenham Examiner* (10 February 1892).
16. Wheaton, B. K., *Victorian Ices & Ice Cream* (The Metropolitan Museum of Art, Charles Scribner's Sons, New York, 1976, USA).
17. *Everyday Housekeeping*, Vol. 6, Issues 2–6 (Home Science Publishing Company, 1896), 181.
18. Marshall, A. B., *Mrs A. B. Marshall's Larger Cookery Book of Extra Recipes* (Marshall's School of Cookery, London, 1902), 36.
19. Ibid., 12.
20. British Newspaper Archive, *Morning Post* (12 December 1887).
21. British Newspaper Archive, *Falkirk Herald* (28 June 1902).
22. Marshall, A. B., *Mrs A. B. Marshall's Larger Cookery Book of Extra Recipes* (Marshall's School of Cookery, London, 1902), 401.
23. Marshall, A. B., *The Book of Ices* (Marshall's School of Cookery, London, 1885), 9.
24. Marshall, A. B., *The Book of Ices* (Marshall's School of Cookery, London, 1885), 11.
25. Marshall, A. B., *Fancy Ices* (Marshall's School of Cookery, London, 1894), v.
26. Ibid., 219–220.
27. Ibid., 215.
28. Bosworth, T., *Anglo-Saxon Dictionary*, https://bosworthtoller.com/52515 (accessed 9 June 2022).
29. Marshall, A. B., *Fancy Ices* (Marshall's School of Cookery, London, 1894), 160.
30. Ranhofer, C., *The Epicurean* (Dover Publications, 2017), 1016.
31. Marshall, A. B., *Fancy Ices* (Marshall's School of Cookery, London, 1894), 135.
32. *The Table* (24 August 1901).

Chapter 3: Isabella Beeton

1. British Newspaper Archive, *Carlisle Journal* (1 August 1840).
2. UK, Land Tax Redemption, 1798 for Isaac Jerom, www.ancestry.co.uk/discoveryui-content/view/483974:2319 (accessed 20 September 2022).

3. London, England, Church of England Births and Baptisms, 1813–1923 for Isaac Jerrom, www.ancestry.co.uk/discoveryui-content/view/154502874:1558?tid=&pid=&queryId=b4c5dd596d1d1b64711d3f7a80f2412e&_phsrc=jzI1222&_phstart=successSource (accessed 20 September 2022).
4. London, England, Church of England Deaths and Burials, 1813–2003 for Isaac Jerrom, www.ancestry.co.uk/discoveryui-content/view/8592932:1559 (accessed 20 September 2022).
5. Proceedings of the Old Bailey online, Robert Owen. Theft: simple larceny, 9 April 1829, www.oldbaileyonline.org/browse.jsp?div=t18290409-53 (accessed 20 September 2022).
6. 1851 England Census for Mary Jerrom, www.ancestry.co.uk/imageviewer/collections/8860/images/KENHO107_1612_1612-0806?treeid=&personid=&hintid=&usePUB=true&usePUBJs=true&pId=1477657 (accessed 20 September 2022).
7. Curran, C., 'Private Women, Public Needs: Middle-Class Widows in Victorian England', *Albion: A Quarterly Journal Concerned with British Studies*, Vol. 25, No. 2 (The North American Conference on British Studies).
8. Cumberland Pacquet, and Ware's Whitehaven Advertiser (16 October 1820).
9. *Morning Herald* (23 May 1863).
10. Harold, J., and Wolff, M., *The Victorian City: Images and Realities: Volume 2* (Routledge, 1999), 460.
11. British Newspaper Archive, *Shipping and Mercantile Gazette* (24 April 1847).
12. British Newspaper Archive, *Morning Post* (29 November 1866).
13. Janet Painter, 'The Dorling Family and Their Connection to Epsom' (2011), *Epsom and Ewell History Explorer*, https://eehe.org.uk/?p=25519 (accessed 5 October 2022).
14. Ibid.
15. Phiz [pseudonym], *The Derby Carnival or London's Greatest Outing* (Ward Lock, London, 1868).
16. Flanagan, B., 'Mrs Beeton and the Book of Household Management', *Friends of West Norwood Cemetery*, Newsletter no. 41, May 2001.
17. *Surrey Advertiser* (29 March 1873).
18. Spain, N., *Mrs Beeton and Her Husband* (Collins, London, 1948), 33–35.

19. Ibid., 67.
20. 1871 England Census for Lucy Dorling, www.ancestry.co.uk/imageviewer/collections/7619/images/SRYRG10_847_848-0292?pId=13533941 (accessed 7 October 2022).
21. Janet Painter, 'The Dorling Family and Their Connection to Epsom' (2011), *Epsom and Ewell History Explorer*, https://eehe.org.uk/?p=25519 (accessed 5 October 2022).
22. *Catalogue of the Library of Congress*, Vol. 5 (Library of Congress, 1872).
23. Dorling, W. G. (ed.), *The American Racing Record and Turf Guide* (New York, 1873).
24. Library of Congress, *Chicago Daily Tribune* (4 May 1879).
25. www.imuseum.im/Olive/APA/IsleofMan/SharedView.Article.aspx?href=TMS%2F1862%2F07%2F26&id=Ar01900&sk=CC25F32B&viewMode=image (accessed 30 October 2022)
26. Jackson, L., 'Maysons and Dorlings Revisited' (2019), *Epsom and Ewell History Explorer*, https://eehe.org.uk/?p=25628 (accessed 5 October 2022).
27. Ibid.
28. Jackson, L., 'George Riddington' (2012), *Epsom and Ewell History Explorer*, https://eehe.org.uk/?p=31224 (accessed 5 October 2022).
29. Freeman, Sarah, *Isabella and Sam: The Story of Mrs Beeton* (Coward, McCann & Geoghegan, 1978), 43.
30. British Newspaper Archive, *Islington Gazette* (2 March 1861).
31. British Newspaper Archive, *Surrey Advertiser* (1 May 1886).
32. Cockman, G. and Marshall, J., *Old Views of Epsom Town* (1988).
33. British Newspaper Archive, *Aberdeen Press and Journal* (9 July 1975).
34. Spain, N., *Mrs Beeton and Her Husband* (Collins, London, 1948), 36.
35. Hughes, K., *The Short Life and Long Times of Mrs Beeton* (HarperCollins, 2005).
36. *The Athenaeum, Journal of English and Foreign Literature, Science and the Fine Arts* (J. Francis, London, 1853).
37. Beeton, I., *The Book of Household Management* (Ward, Lock & Company, 1888), 1283.
38. Montgomery Hyde, H., *Mr and Mrs Beeton* (George G. Harrop & Co. Ltd, London, Sydney, Toronto, Bombay, 1951), 103.
39. Spain, N., *Mrs Beeton and Her Husband* (Collins, London, 1948).

40. Freeman, Sarah, *Isabella and Sam: The Story of Mrs Beeton* (Coward, McCann & Geoghegan, 1978), 110.
41. Ibid., 119.
42. *The Times* (3 February 1932).
43. Ward, M., '"A Charm in Those Fingers": Patterns, Taste, and the Englishwoman's Domestic Magazine', *Victorian Periodicals Review*, Vol. 41, No. 3 (John Hopkins University Press, 2008).
44. Broomfield, A., 'Rushing Dinner to the Table: The "Englishwoman's Domestic Magazine" and Industrialization's Effects on Middle-Class Food and Cooking, 1852–1860', *Victorian Periodicals Review*, Vol. 41, No. 2 (John Hopkins University Press, 2008).
45. 1861 England Census for Isabella M. Beeton, www.ancestry.co.uk/imageviewer/collections/8767/images/BRKRG9_782_783-0395?pId=10942274 (accessed 10 November 2021).
46. Flanagan, B., 'Mrs Beeton and the Book of Household Management', *Friends of West Norwood Cemetery*, Newsletter no. 41, May 2001.
47. *The Villager*, xi. 'A History of the County of Middlesex: Volume 4, Harmondsworth, Hayes, Norwood With Southall, Hillingdon With Uxbridge, Ickenham, Northolt, Perivale, Ruislip, Edgware, Harrow With Pinner' (originally published Victoria County History, London, 1971).
48. Sotheby's L11408, Lot 5, Beeton, Isabella. www.sothebys.com/en/auctions/ecatalogue/2011/english-literature-history-private-press-childrens-books-illustrations/lot.5.html (accessed 20 November 2022).
49. Montgomery Hyde, H., *Mr and Mrs Beeton* (George G. Harrop & Co. Ltd, London, Sydney, Toronto, Bombay, 1951), 115.
50. British Newspaper Archive, *Dundee Courier* (22 January 1947).
51. British Newspaper Archive, *Yorkshire Evening Post* (15 November 1947).
52. Davis, L. S., *A Polar Affair* (Simon & Schuster, 2019).
53. British Newspaper Archive, *Dundee Courier* (10 July 1914).
54. UK and Ireland, Outward Passenger Lists, 1890–1960 for Isabel Cecile Beeton, www.ancestry.co.uk/imageviewer/collections/2997/images/40610_B001170-00361?pId=47405540 (accessed 7 October 2022).

55. 1891 England Census for Matilda Brown, www.ancestry.co.uk/discoveryui-content/view/18253743:6598 (accessed 7 October 2022).
56. Proceedings of the Old Bailey online, James Fitzgerald. Theft: stealing from master, 17 August 1835, www.oldbaileyonline.org/browse.jsp?div=t18350817-1852 (accessed 20 September 2022).
57. *The Pall Mall Budget*, Vol. 18 (Kellet, London, 1869).
58. James, Louis, '"Now Inhale the Gas": Interactive Readership in Two Victorian Boys' Periodicals, 1855–1870', *Victorian Periodicals Review*, Vol. 42, No. 1 (Johns Hopkins University Press).
59. Lambie, James, *The Story of Your Life* (Matador, Leicester, 2010).
60. Ibid., 28–29.
61. British Newspaper Archive, *Belfast Newsletter* (2 December 1879).
62. Spain, N., *Mrs Beeton and Her Husband* (Collins, London, 1948), 61.
63. *Public Opinion: A Weekly Review of Current Thought and Activity* (London, 1866)
64. Spain, N., *Mrs Beeton and Her Husband* (Collins, London, 1948), 67.
65. Benainous, R., Alunji, M., Brillet, P., and Dhote, R., *Pulmonary Involvement in Secondary Syphilis* (*EJCRIM*, 2021).
66. British Newspaper Archive, *Illustrated Times* (18 February 1865).

Chapter 4: The *Book of Household Management* and Other Stories

1. Sanders, Valerie (ed.), *Harriet Martineau: Selected Letters* (Clarendon Press, Oxford, 1990), 200.
2. Beeton, I., *The Book of Household Management* (S. O. Beeton, London, 1866), 190.
3. Gregory, James, 'Veggie Victorians: how Britain responded to the rise of the meat-free movement', 2018, *History Extra*, www.historyextra.com/period/victorian/veggie-victorians (accessed 21 October 2022).
4. Beeton, I., *The Book of Household Management* (S. O. Beeton, London, 1861), 64.
5. Ibid., 637.
6. Beck, John, *Beck's, 'Late Fairfax's', Leamington Guide* (J. Beck, Leamington Spa, 1839).

7. Beeton, I., *The Book of Household Management* (S. O. Beeton, London, 1866), 221.
8. *Oddfellows' Magazine*, Vol. 3 (G. M. and Board of Directors, 1862, Manchester).
9. British Newspaper Archive, *Oxford Journal* (11 October 1828).
10. Beeton, I., *The Book of Household Management* (S. O. Beeton, London, 1866), 395.
11. Ibid., 906.
12. Ibid., 667.
13. Ibid., 720.
14. Ibid., 68.
15. British Newspaper Archive, *The Era* (10 March 1850).
16. Beeton, I., *The Book of Household Management* (S. O. Beeton, London, 1866), 636.
17. Ibid., 712.
18. Ibid., 100.
19. Marshall, A., *Mrs A. B. Marshall's Cookery Book* (Simpkin, Marshall, Hamilton, Kent & Co. Ltd, London, 1890), 115.
20. Gouffe, Jules, *The Royal Cookery Book* (Sampson Low, Son, and Marston, 1869, London), 234.
21. Beeton, I., *The Book of Household Management* (S. O. Beeton, London, 1866), 99.
22. British Newspaper Archive, *New Times (London)* (26 January 1820).
23. Beeton, I., *The Book of Household Management* (S. O.Beeton, London, 1861), 479.
24. Beeton, I., *The Book of Household Management* (S. O.Beeton, London, 1861), 350.
25. Soyer, Alexis, *The Modern Housewife, Or Menagere* (D. Appleton & Company, New York, 1850), 116.
26. Beeton, I., *The Book of Household Management* (S. O.Beeton, London, 1861), 307.
27. Ibid., 670.
28. Ibid., 314.
29. British Newspaper Archive, *Derby Mercury* (24 February 1841).
30. Beeton, I., *The Book of Household Management* (S. O. Beeton, London, 1861), 630.
31. Ibid., 667.

32. Wilson, Mrs Henry Lumpkin, *Tested Recipe Cook Book* (The Foote & Davies Company, Atlanta, 1805), 82.
33. Beeton, I., *Englishwoman's Domestic Magazine*, Vol. 5 (S. O. Beeton, London, 1857), 374.
34. Beeton, I., *The Englishwoman's Domestic Magazine*, Vols. 5–6 (S. O. Beeton, London, 1857), 32.
35. Ibid., 345.
36. Acton, E., *Modern Cookery for Private Families* (Longmans, Green and Company, 1865), 558.
37. Beeton, I., *The Englishwoman's Domestic Magazine*, Vols. 5–6 (S. O. Beeton, London, 1857), 93.
38. Beeton, I., *The Englishwoman's Domestic Magazine 1852–1862*, Vol. 7 (S. O. Beeton, London), 63.
39. Beeton, I., *The Book of Household Management* (S. O.Beeton, London, 1861), 892.
40. Austen, Jane, *Mansfield Park* (Derby & Jackson, New York, 1860), 255.
41. Dickens, C., *Charles Dickens Works* (G. W. Dillingham, New York, 1885), 35.
42. Dickens, C., *Christmas Stories* (Estes and Lauriat, Boston, 1883), 57.
43. Thackeray, W.M., *Vanity Fair* (Leipzig, 1848).
44. Beeton, I., *The Book of Household Management* (S. O. Beeton, London, 1861), 890.
45. Pennant, T., *A Tour in Scotland*, 1769, Volume 2 (B. White at Horace's Head, London), 94.
46. Beeton, I., *The Book of Household Management* (S. O.Beeton, London, 1861), 900.

Chapter 5: Day-to-Day Lives, Pinner and Peers

1. Stuart-Bennet, J. G., *Motherhood, Respectability and Baby-Farming in Victorian and Edwardian London* (Routledge, Oxford, 2023).
2. *A Short History of London's Buses*, London Transport Museum, www.ltmuseum.co.uk/collections/stories/transport/short-history-londons-buses (accessed 12 November 2022).
3. Pinner Local History Society, *Around Pinner* (Amberley Publishing, Stroud, 2013), 70.

4. Pinner Local History Society, *Around Pinner* (Amberley Publishing, Stroud, 2013).
5. Kay, Emma, *Vintage Kitchenalia* (Amberley Publishing, Stroud, 2017).
6. Dickens, C., *A Tale of Two Cities* (Chapman & Hall, London, 1868).
7. Kay, E., *Dining with the Victorians* (Amberley Publishing, Stroud, 2015).
8. Francatelli, C. E., *A Plain Cookery Book for the Working Classes* (London, 1852).
9. Kay, E., *Cooking Up History: Chefs of the Past* (Prospect Books, London, 2017).
10. Wright, C. E. Guthrie, *The School Cookery Book* (Macmillan, London, 1881), 87.
11. Kay, E., *Cooking Up History: Chefs of the Past* (Prospect Books, London, 2017).

Bibliography

Acton, E., *Modern Cookery in All Its Branches* (Lea and Blanchard, Philadelphia and London, 1845).

Acton, E., *Modern Cookery for Private Families* (Longmans, Green and Company, 1865).

A Short History of London's Buses, London Transport Museum, www.ltmuseum.co.uk/collections/stories/transport/short-history-londons-buses (accessed 12 November 2022).

Austen, J., *Mansfield Park* (Derby & Jackson, New York, 1860).

Beeton, I., *The Englishwoman's Domestic Magazine*, Vol. 5 (S. O. Beeton, London, 1857).

Beeton, I., *The Englishwoman's Domestic Magazine* 1852–1862, Vol. 7 (S. O. Beeton, London).

Beck, John, *Beck's, 'Late Fairfax's', Leamington Guide* (J. Beck, Leamington Spa, 1839).

Beeton, I., *The Book of Household Management* (S. O. Beeton, London, 1861).

Beeton, I., *The Book of Household Management* (S. O. Beeton, London, 1866).

Beeton, I., *The Book of Household Management* (Ward, Lock & Company, 1888).

Benainous, R., Alunji, M., Brillet, P., and Dhote, R., 'Pulmonary Involvement in Secondary Syphilis' (*EJCRIM*, 2021).

Bosworth, T., *Anglo-Saxon Dictionary*, https://bosworthtoller.com/52515 (accessed 9 June 2022).

Broomfield, A., 'Rushing Dinner to the Table: The "Englishwoman's Domestic Magazine" and Industrialization's Effects on Middle-Class Food and Cooking, 1852–1860', *Victorian Periodicals Review*, Vol. 41, No. 2 (Johns Hopkins University Press, 2008).

Catalogue of the Library of Congress, Vol. 5 (Library of Congress, 1872).

Cockman, G., and Marshall, J., *Old Views of Epsom Town* (1988).
Craddock, F., *The Sherlock Holmes Cookbook* (W. H. Allen, London, 1976).
Curran, C., 'Private Women, Public Needs: Middle-Class Widows in Victorian England', *Albion: A Quarterly Journal Concerned with British Studies*, Vol. 25, No. 2 (The North American Conference on British Studies).
Current Opinion (The Current Literature Publishing Co., New York, 1894).
Davis, L. S., *A Polar Affair* (Simon & Schuster, 2019).
Dickens, C., *A Tale of Two Cities* (Chapman & Hall, London, 1868).
Dickens, C., *Charles Dickens Works* (G. W. Dillingham, New York, 1885).
Dickens, C., *Christmas Stories* (Estes and Lauriat, Boston, 1883).
Deith, J., *The Greatest Victorian Ice Cream Maker* (Smith Settle Ltd, Yorkshire, 1998).
De Ridder, J., and Van Remoortel, M., 'Not "Simply Mrs. Warren": Eliza Warren Francis (1810–1900) and the "Ladies' Treasury"', *Victorian Periodicals Review*, Vol. 44, No. 4 (The Johns Hopkins University Press, 2011).
Dorling, W. G. (ed.), *The American Racing Record and Turf Guide* (New York, 1873).
Everyday Housekeeping, Vol. 6, Issues 2–6 (Home Science Publishing Company, 1896).
Flanagan, B., 'Mrs Beeton and the *Book of Household Management*', *Friends of West Norwood Cemetery*, Newsletter no. 41, May 2001.
Francatelli, C. E., *The Modern Cook* (T. B.Peterson, 1877).
Freeman, S., *Isabella and Sam: The Story of Mrs Beeton* (Coward, McCann & Geoghegan, 1978).
Freeman, S., *The Story of Mrs Beeton* (Victor Gollancz LTD, London).
Geddes, K., *Keep Calm and Fanny On! The Many Careers of Fanny Craddock* (Fantom Publishing, Croydon, 2019).
Glasse, H., *The Complete Confectioner* (West and Hughes, London, 1800).
Gouffe, J., *The Royal Cookery Book* (Sampson Low, Son, and Marston, 1869, London).
Gregory, J., 'Veggie Victorians: how Britain responded to the rise of the meat-free movement', 2018, *History Extra*, www.historyextra.com/period/victorian/veggie-victorians (accessed 21 October 2022).

Harold, J., and Wolff, M., *The Victorian City: Images and Realities*, Volume 2 (Routledge, London, 1999).

Hughes, K., *The Short Life and Long Times of Mrs Beeton* (HarperCollins, London, 2005).

James, L., '"Now Inhale the Gas": Interactive Readership in Two Victorian Boys' Periodicals, 1855–1870', *Victorian Periodicals Review*, Vol. 42, No. 1 (Johns Hopkins University Press).

Jerome, J. K. (ed.), *To-Day: A Weekly Magazine-Journal*, Vol. 7 (Howard House, London, 1895).

Karsland, V., *Women and Their Work* (Sampson Low, Marston & Company, London, 1891).

Kay, E., *Cooking up History: Chefs of the Past* (Prospect Books, London, 2017).

Kay, E., *Dining with the Georgians* (Amberley Publishing, Stroud, 2014).

Kay, E., *Vintage Kitchenalia* (Amberley Publishing, Stroud, 2017).

Kitchiner, W., *The Cook's Oracle* (London, 1827).

Lambie, J., *The Story of Your Life* (Matador, Leicester, 2010).

Larousse Gastronomique (Paul Hamlyn Ltd, London, 1961).

Marshall, A. B., *Fancy Ices* (Marshall's School of Cookery, London, 1894).

Marshall, A., *Mrs A. B. Marshall's Cookery Book* (Simpkin, Marshall, Hamilton, Kent & Co. Ltd, London, 1890).

Marshall, A. B., *Mrs A. B. Marshall's Larger Cookery Book of Extra Recipes* (Marshall's School of Cookery, London, 1902).

Marshall, A. B., *The Book of Ices* (Marshall's School of Cookery, London, 1885).

Mason, C., *The Lady's Assistant for Regulating and Supplying the Table* (C. Whittington, London, 1801).

Montgomery Hyde, H., *Mr and Mrs Beeton* (George G. Harrop & Co. Ltd, London, Sydney, Toronto, Bombay, 1951).

Oddfellows' Magazine, Vol. 3 (G. M. and Board of Directors, 1862, Manchester).

Parliament, Great Britain, House of Commons, *Accounts and Papers of the House of Commons*, Vol. 41 (London, 1862).

Pennant, T., *A Tour in Scotland*, Vol. 2 (B. White at Horace's Head, London, 1769).

Plat, H., *Delights for Ladies* (Robert Young, London, 1636).

Phiz [pseudonym], *The Derby Carnival or London's Greatest Outing* (Ward Lock, London, 1868).

Pinner Local History Society, *Around Pinner* (Amberley Publishing, Stroud, 2013).

Public Opinion: A Weekly Review of Current Thought and Activity (London, 1866).

Ranhofer, C., *The Epicurean* (Dover Publications, 2017).

Sanders, V. (ed.), *Harriet Martineau: Selected Letters* (Clarendon Press, Oxford, 1990), 200.

Soyer, A., *The Modern Housewife, Or Menagere* (D. Appleton & Company, New York, 1850).

Spain, N., *Mrs Beeton and Her Husband* (Collins, London, 1948).

Stuart-Bennet, J. G., *Motherhood, Respectability and Baby-Farming in Victorian and Edwardian London* (Routledge, Oxford, 2023).

Talbot, V. A., *What to Do with Our Girls; or, Employments for Women* (Houlston & Sons, London, 1884).

Thackeray, W. M., *Vanity Fair* (Leipzig, 1848).

The Athenaeum, Journal of English and Foreign Literature, Science and the Fine Arts (J. Francis, London, 1853).

The Gas World, Vol. 18 (John Allan, London, 1893).

The Lady's Realm, Vol. XI, November 1901 to April 1902 (Hutchinson and Co., London, 1902).

The Lancet (1885), 34.

The Pall Mall Budget, Vol. 18 (Kellet, London, 1869).

The Table, June 1886.

The Table, 24 August 1901.

The Villager, xi. 'A History of the County of Middlesex: Volume 4, Harmondsworth, Hayes, Norwood With Southall, Hillingdon With Uxbridge, Ickenham, Northolt, Perivale, Ruislip, Edgware, Harrow With Pinner' (originally published by Victoria County History, London, 1971).

Theodore, F. G., The Encyclopædia of Practical Cookery: A Complete Dictionary of All Pertaining to the Art of Cookery and Table Service (Upcott Gill, London, 1892).

Truth, Vol. 33: January–June (London, 1893).

Van Lieshout, C., 'Portrait of a lady: the female entrepreneur in England and Wales, 1851–1911', London School of Economics (2019), https://

blogs.lse.ac.uk/businessreview/2019/05/17/portrait-of-a-lady-the-female-entrepreneur-in-england-and-wales-1851-1911 (accessed 7 October 2021).

Ward, M., '"A Charm in Those Fingers": Patterns, Taste, and the Englishwoman's Domestic Magazine', *Victorian Periodicals Review*, Vol. 41, No. 3 (Johns Hopkins University Press, 2008).

Wheaton, B. K., *Victorian Ices & Ice Cream* (The Metropolitan Museum of Art, Charles Scribner's Sons, New York, 1976).

Wilson, H. L., *Tested Recipe Cook Book* (The Foote & Davies Company, Atlanta, 1805).

Wright, C. E. Guthrie, *The School Cookery Book* (Macmillan, London, 1881).

Websites

British Newspaper Archive: britishnewspaperarchive.co.uk

    British Newspaper Archive, *Cardiff Times* (12 February 1887).

    British Newspaper Archive, *Pall Mall Gazette* (14 October 1886).

    British Newspaper Archive, *The Uxbridge & W. Drayton Gazette* (5 August 1905).

    British Newspaper Archive, *Daily Telegraph & Courier* (London) (1 September 1911).

    British Newspaper Archive, *Brighton Gazette* (5 May 1853).

    British Newspaper Archive, *Ludlow Advertiser* (27 October 1900).

    British Newspaper Archive, *Ludlow Advertiser* (7 May 1904).

    British Newspaper Archive, *Kensington Post* (10 March 1961).

    British Newspaper Archive, *The Edinburgh Gazette* (22 April 1924).

    British Newspaper Archive, *The Daily Telegraph* (27 February 1904).

    British Newspaper Archive, *Harrow Observer* (19 June 1908).

    British Newspaper Archive, *Uxbridge & W. Drayton Gazette* (1 October 1904).

    British Newspaper Archive, *West London Observer* (6 September 1935).

    British Newspaper Archive, *London Evening Standard* (3 December 1913).

    British Newspaper Archive, *Lloyd's Weekly Newspaper* (14 February 1897).

    British Newspaper Archive, *Harrow Observer* (8 July 1910).

    British Newspaper Archive, *The Cheltenham Examiner* (2 August 1905).

    British Newspaper Archive, *Harrow Observer* (17 July 1914).

    British Newspaper Archive, *Aldershot Military Gazette* (12 April 1879).

British Newspaper Archive, *Harrow Observer* (5 October 1906).
British Newspaper Archive, *Harrow Observer* (23 July 1897).
British Newspaper Archive, *Harrow Observer* (23 February 1917).
British Newspaper Archive, *Morning Post* (14 November 1883).
British Newspaper Archive, *Pall Mall Gazette* (14 October 1886).
British Newspaper Archive, *Cheltenham Examiner* (27 October 1886).
British Newspaper Archive, *The Queen* (13 April 1895).
British Newspaper Archive, *The Queen* (17 February 1900).
British Newspaper Archive, *The Queen*, Saturday (23 June 1900).
British Newspaper Archive, *The Queen*, Saturday (13 June 1903).
British Newspaper Archive, *The Queen*, Saturday (4 July 1903).
British Newspaper Archive, *The Queen*, Saturday (30 March 1895).
British Newspaper Archive, *The Queen*, Saturday (19 May 1894).
British Newspaper Archive, Edinburgh Evening News (28 April 1925).
British Newspaper Archive, *The Queen*, Saturday (13 April 189), 5.
British Newspaper Archive, *Morning Post* (30 January 1893).
British Newspaper Archive, *Pall Mall Gazette* (14 October 1886).
British Newspaper Archive, *Pall Mall Gazette* (18 May 1895).
British Newspaper Archive, *Pall Mall Gazette* (5 May 1888).
British Newspaper Archive, *Birmingham Daily Post* (10 August 1887).
British Newspaper Archive, *Newcastle Daily Chronicle* (22 September 1892).
British Newspaper Archive, *Hull Daily Mail* (10 January 1893).
British Newspaper Archive, *Dundee Advertiser* (28 September 1892).
British Newspaper Archive, *Truth* (15 September 1892).
British Newspaper Archive, *Truth* (17 August 1905).
British Newspaper Archive, *The Dundee Advertiser* (28 September 1892).
British Newspaper Archive, *Cardiff Times* (12 February 1887).
British Newspaper Archive, *Morning Post* (12 December 1887).
British Newspaper Archive, *The Cheltenham Examiner* (2 August 1905).
British Newspaper Archive, *The Yorkshire* Post (1 November 1886).
British Newspaper Archive, *Cheltenham Examiner* (10 February 1892).
British Newspaper Archive, *Truth* (13 July 1893).
British Newspaper Archive, *Morning Post* (12 December 1887).
British Newspaper Archive, *Falkirk Herald* (28 June 1902).
British Newspaper Archive, *Cumberland Pacquet, and Ware's Whitehaven Advertiser* (16 October 1820).

Bibliography

British Newspaper Archive, *Sporting Life* (6 August 1862).
British Newspaper Archive, *Morning Herald* (23 May 1863).
British Newspaper Archive, *Shipping and Mercantile Gazette* (24 April 1847).
British Newspaper Archive, *Morning Post* (29 November 1866).
British Newspaper Archive, *Surrey Advertiser* (29 March 1873).
British Newspaper Archive, *Myra's Journal of Dress and Fashion* (1 May 1892).
British Newspaper Archive, *Lisburn Standard* (5 March 1904).
British Newspaper Archive, *Islington Gazette* (2 March 1861).
British Newspaper Archive, *West Surrey Times* (1 May 1886).
British Newspaper Archive, *Surrey Advertiser* (1 May 1886).
British Newspaper Archive, *Aberdeen Press and Journal* (9 July 1975).
British Newspaper Archive, *Dundee Courier* (22 January 1947).
British Newspaper Archive, *Yorkshire Evening Post* (15 November 1947).
British Newspaper Archive, *Illustrated Sporting News and Theatrical and Musical Review* (7 November 1868).
British Newspaper Archive, *Illustrated Times* (18 February 1865).
British Newspaper Archive, *New Times (London)* (26 January 1820).
British Newspaper Archive, *Derby Mercury* (24 February 1841).

Library of Congress, Chronicling America: Historic American Newspapers: chroniclingamerica.loc.gov/search/pages/results/?state=&date1=1836&date2=1922&proxtext=cooking&x=0&y=0&dateFilterType=yearRange&rows=20&searchType=basic

The Times Newspaper Archives online: www.thetimes.co.uk/archive
Ancestry: ancestry.co.uk
The Proceedings of The Old Bailey: oldbaileyonline.org
Pinner Local History Society: www.pinnerlhs.org.uk
Google Patents: patents.google.com
Epsom and Ewell History Explorer: eehe.org.uk
i.Museum: www.imuseum.im
London Transport Museum: *A Short History of London's Buses*, London Transport Museum, www.ltmuseum.co.uk/collections/stories/transport/short-history-londons-buses (accessed 12 November 2022).
Sotheby's: www.sothebys.com